GIRLS SPEAK OUT

GIRLS SPEAK OUT

Finding Your True Self

Andrea Johnston

Foreword by Gloria Steinem

Celestial Arts
Box 7123
Berkeley, California 94707
www.tenspeed.com

Distributed in Australia by Simon and Schuster Australia, in Canada by Ten Speed Press Canada, in New Zealand by Southern Publishers Group, in South Africa by Real Books, and in the United Kingdom and Europe by Airlift Book Company.

Cover design by Rebecca Neimark
Text design by Tasha Hall
Illustrations by Dan Krovatin
Front cover image by Justin Pumfrey/Getty Images

For further acknowledgments, please see pages 222–23.

Library of Congress Cataloging-in-Publication Data
Johnston, Andrea.
Girls speak out : finding your true self / Andrea Johnston ; foreword by Gloria Steinem.—2nd ed.
p. cm.
Includes bibliographical references and index.
ISBN-10: 1-58761-241-0
ISBN-13: 978-1-58761-241-1
1. Teenage girls—United States—Psychology—Juvenile literature. 2. Self-esteem in adolescence—United States—Juvenile literature. 3. Self-perception in adolescence—United States—Juvenile literature. 4. Self-esteem in women—United States—Juvenile literature. 5. Self-help groups—Activity programs—Juvenile literature. I. Title.

HQ798.J615 2005
158.1'0835'2—dc22

2005001270

Printed in the United States of America
First printing this edition, 2005

1 2 3 4 5 6 7 8 9 10 — 09 08 07 06 05

To Jesse and Yulahlia, in honor of their
truth-gazing, hearts, and optimism, and for teaching me to trust.

And to girls and their friends everywhere,
in appreciation of their vision, hope, and faith in each of us.

Contents

Acknowledgments

When Gloria Steinem and I decided to create a program for girls, we had no idea it would grow into its own international movement to help empower them. Originally, we wanted to use prehistory to show other possibilities for female human beings. In order to make that idea come alive in girls' hands, I asked some friends to form a steering committee. We met in my house for about six months.

Four ex-students of mine became steering-committee teachers while they were in middle school: Christina Dry, Elizabeth "Lizard" Foster-Shaner, Meghan Long, and Sarah Mascolo talked, listened, laughed, read, sewed, ate, shopped, hiked, field-tested artifacts, and kept journals so we could give other girls what they would like to experience. Nine-year-old Emily Luna and nineteen-year-old Pauline Greenfield also joined the group. Memories of their enthusiasm have inspired me through the years.

In September 1994, we were ready to leave my house and go on the road. Our original name for the program was Talks for Girls, a name that traveled with me until we realized that Talks for Girls was too similar to other names already in circulation. My agent and lawyer, Bob Levine, asked his then ten-year-old daughter, Joanna, a program participant, to brainstorm with us. I'm grateful to Joanna for thinking of Girls Speak Out. She is off to college, and Bob remains the best role model of a dedicated feminist. Pauline Marsilis at Levine, Plotkin and Menin is a steadfast friend of Girls Speak Out.

Pia Hamilton became a certified teacher, and Jan Moore left and returned to public school teaching as we developed Girls Speak Out. Francine Kuney shared her concern for her grandchildren's future, and until her recent death, she promoted the program and believed in the power of this book. Retired school librarian Milly Lee sold her first children's book as she looked for books for Girls Speak Out, and today her third book is ready for publication. (Her updated list of recommended books is at the back of this book.) Milly is a tireless advocate for children, and it is a joy to be friends with her and her husband, Kearn. Thankfully, Gail Dry, Christina's mother, has never left the side of Girls Speak Out.

After leaving my house, I met women who shared their expertise. Jean Shinoda Bolen, MD, brainstormed about how we could be sure Girls Speak Out is a safe place for girls. Hallie Iglehart Austen searched for artifacts and brought the steering committee to her backyard labyrinth in Point Reyes, California.

Our first pilot program was held in our backyard, in Sonoma County, California, where the steering committe teachers and I lived. We soon traveled to the San Jose, California YWCA, and then-principal Virginia McQueen brought students from her San Jose school. Kristina Kiehl and her daughter, Annie, were among our earliest and warmest supporters. Amelia Richards, one of the founders of Third Wave, a nationwide organization of young feminists, and coauthor of *Manifesta* and *Grassroots: A Field Guide to Feminist Activism*, organized Girls Speak Out's third and fourth pilot programs in the Third Wave offices in New York City.

The Ms. Foundation for Women is one of the first collective voices for girls and women heard in this country, and with its help, Girls Speak Out was ready to travel extensively.

Tara Tremmel is one of Girls Speak Out's earliest wise women; she traveled with me to different states, videotaped hundreds of girls, and opened her heart to all of us.

Photographer Jennifer Warburg went from state to state, carrying more equipment than anyone should, in record-breaking heat and cold, to capture the range of feeling in the faces of the girls and women who've participated in the program.

Gail Maynor brought her joy—and her Girl Scout troop—to the Ms. Foundation's offices for Girls Speak Out sessions. We are fortunate to have Gail's faith as part of our foundation. In 1995, Girls Speak Out affiliated with the YWCA of the USA for a year to ensure that sessions would be held in female-friendly places across the USA. As I visited different YWCAs, I began to realize why Gloria and other feminists who work on a grassroots level are optimistic about what's happening in the women's movement. The women who organized sessions and worked with me at the following YWCA locations were an inspiration and a joy: I thank the staff and volunteers in Chicago, Illinois; Minneapolis, Minnesota; San Diego, California; Portland, Oregon; Charleston, South Carolina; and Wheeling, West Virginia.

Girls Speak Out sessions have also been held in public housing developments. The I Have a Dream program in Chelsea-Elliot public housing became a Girls Speak Out site through the efforts of Kathleen Clarke-Glover, then director of the Office of Education, New York City Public Housing, and Roberta Stallings, her then chief of staff.

Today Girls Speak Out has a new training and certification program for workshop organizers and leaders. The YWCA Toronto has been a blessing to work with as we piloted a successful model program in Canada (see guide at the back of this book). Amy Brooks, YWCA Teen Mothers' Program Worker; Pauline Paterson, YWCA Manager of Family and Child Support Services;

Sara Ramnarine, YWCA Girl's Night Program Worker; and Sally Palmateer, YWCA Director, Counseling, Education and Group Work, have made it possible for women across YWCAs in Canada to come together, experience the program, and then return home to spread its message across the country.

Girls Speak Out inspired me to travel back to my own childhood, and I was fortunate to find people I felt and heard as a young girl who still speak from the heart. My cousin Marianne "Bunny" Cairo; Arlene Gold, my seventh- and eighth-grade teacher; and Eleanor Ehrenkranz, my high school teacher and a mentor, prove to me that if we look deep inside ourselves, we'll find love. I thank my mother for listening, even after she realized I was never good at keeping secrets. My nephews, Pedrito, Daniel, and Peter, continue to make me glad I live in the present. My brother, Stephen, sister, Janie, and sister-in-law, Debbie, have established a tradition of working for children that is essential to a new beginning for our family.

I'm continually grateful for the guidance of agent Felicia Eth because, among other things, she champions whistle-blowers. Her attempts to educate the publishing world about sexual harassment in the schools, even as my book proposal on that topic received rejection after rejection, were instrumental in breaking down the walls of isolation I was experiencing in my local community. Today her daughters are also benefiting from her insights into female power.

Brenda Bowen, vice president and editor-in-chief at Hyperion Books, listened to my inchoate pitch when she was an editor at Scholastic and captured the heart of Girls Speak Out for the first edition of this book. Countless benefits flow from her sky's-the-limit philosophy.

Alice Walker's generosity, support, and storytelling are touchstones in more ways than are visible in this book. Joan Miura is, among many things, Alice's assistant, and she is a generous and steady spirit. I thank Anita Hill for reminding me of "magic" and that change takes patience. Marcia Ann Gillespie helped me to understand that being in the moment means listening to my own voice. Clarissa Pinkola Estés focused me inward at a time when I was struggling to be all things to all people, and she held the standard of inner peace too high for me to miss.

Ted Turner opened his ranch, Vermejo, where he restored nature to its glory, to my niece and I, and we experienced a rare opportunity to simplify, refocus, and revel in each day. He also insisted that a book could be spiritually *and* financially viable.

I am grateful to Dr. Maya Angelou for allowing me to move forward with Girls Speak Out's new project (collecting and publishing writings of girls in juvenile detention centers and jails) with the inspirational name, The Caged Bird Sings.

Misrak Elias of UNICEF shared her expertise on gender issues worldwide, and I am grateful for her perspective and support of Girls Speak Out and the First National Girls' Conference. The children and families of Jordan and South Africa are fortunate that she was the UNICEF ambassador to their countries. The United Nations Global Teaching and Learning Project (www.cyberschoolbus.un.org) is on the cutting edge of educating youth and their elders. Its projects help make it possible for girls' voices to resonate in many languages on the global stage, which is where girls belong.

The Girls' Middle School in Mountain View, California, is a model private school with a commitment to girls' self-reliance and diversity. The girls, staff, board, donors, founder, and parents have achieved an extraordinary goal: girls in school from a wide variety of backgrounds are happy, vibrant, and strong at a critical time in their lives. I enjoy helping make that happen for a variety of girls in Silicon Valley.

Kamala Harris, the first woman district attorney in San Francisco's history and the first African-American woman to hold that office, is a true activist for girls. I hope to visit her in the White House. Norma Hotaling, the founder of SAGE (Standing Against Global Exploitation), worked to make the Secure House for abandoned girls in San Francisco a reality by building on her own activist history. When I suggested we characterize the facility and its program as "secure" rather than safe, Norma and Kamala became its voice.

Amy Laughlin—mother, philanthropist, and children's book author—organized supporters to promote Girls Speak Out and me, and I was lucky to find her at a critical time in my professional life.

Jane Fonda spoke up to bring me to her Georgia program, G-CAPP (the Georgia Campaign for Adolescence Pregnancy Prevention), where I reconnected with coed workshops. In Jane, I found an advocate who follows her inner voice and keeps it focused on liberating victims of injustice.

Carole and Bruce Hart helped create *Sesame Street* and *Free to Be . . .* and, luckily, they wanted the message in Girls Speak Out to reach as many girls as possible, too. As we move in the direction they foresaw, I am excited about the good we can accomplish through their largesse and vision.

I was fortunate when Julie Bennett answered the phone six years ago and listened to my dreams for girls. Now she is this book's editor and champion, and a friend. Her perseverance kept the vision of this edition alive. The girls we will reach thank her, too.

Friends on both coasts continue to come together to keep Girls Speak Out, and me, moving: Cindy Tew has stood by when times were tough; I'm glad we both emerged stronger, and that I met some terrific Southern women and girls along the way. Virginia McDonald (Aunt Gin) has grace and a righteous anger that lights up Harlem and illuminates life. Grace Woodard's love of nature and the art of screenwriting have led me in new directions. Judy Weston-Thompson allows me to hear myself, to listen to others, and to have faith.

Martha Baker is proof to me of past lives, because when we met, it was as sisters with a long, shared history. Martha gives me shelter in countless ways. Bella Abzug made it possible for girls to come to the United Nations for the First National Girls' Conference, and she fought for that victory with her inimitable humor and unflappable conviction.

Girls' voices move me faster and farther than I imagine anyone can travel. Amulya in India, Nailoke and Alisha in Namibia, Sydelle in New York City, and Tiffany and Monica in Northern California are on wonderful journeys. Anna Padarath is the Young Women's Officer of the Fiji Women's Rights Movement in Suva, Fiji, and the efforts of her organization to educate and liberate females are life changing. The interest, strength, and authentic joy of these young women in making things better for girls and women bode well for our future.

Marlo Thomas's spirit and her commitment to *Free to Be . . .* make me smile and keep on going. She responds to Girls Speak Out with the same grace and generosity she embodies in her acting and in her dedication to St. Jude Children's Research Hospital. Marlo embodies the titles of her books, *The Right Words at the Right Time* and *Thanks and Giving All Year Long.*

Gloria Steinem is a lifelong parent of Girls Speak Out and at times, she gives it and me a home. She had a better idea of what we were getting into, and thank the goddess we keep on going. She shows me that fundamental change takes stamina and comes from the heart. Gloria is fearless, ageless, and honest. I hope this book is blessed with some of her spirit.

My niece and goddess-daughter, Yulahlia, is the goddessmother of Girls Speak Out. She participated in sessions, she inspires young girls who want to be their true selves, as she is, and she expands the focus of Girls Speak Out—and my life—with her insights. I'm proud she's a lawyer and that she continually reaches beyond her grasp. Viva Puerto Rico!

My feminist son, Jesse, alternately advises me to "get over yourself," and trust my instincts in keeping Girls Speak Out alive. Sometimes this meant risking where and how we lived for the sake of what he believes: that everyone matters. His generosity and wisdom amaze me. Go Niners!

Thank you, universe and parents, supporters, and guardians, for sharing your daughters.

Thank you, girls, for being you.

Foreword by Gloria Steinem

This book is for every girl who wants to find her true self, and for every friend of a girl who wants to help her. It's also a good book for grown-ups who work with girls, and for women who want to rediscover the girl who lives inside them.

Because a book is like a person, I'd like to tell you the story of how this book came to be:

I am a feminist organizer. That means I travel around the country, trying to help people who want to create more fairness for girls and women—which makes life better for boys and men, too. Sometimes the people are inside families or in schools, sometimes in the workplace or in our political system. I've been doing this for a very long time, longer than most of you reading this have been alive and maybe longer than your parents have been alive, so I've learned a lot.

I've learned that each person is important, and so is everything that happens to each person. In fact, a pretty good first step to almost any kind of change is looking at the world as if everyone mattered. That's because most problems in the world seem to come from one group of people pretending to be superior to another, not because of how hard they worked, but whether they were born male instead of female, or white instead of the many other colors people come in, or rich instead of poor.

I've learned that we can do a lot more if we find people who believe in us, and talk to them as often as we can.

And I've learned for sure that girls like you already have a unique strength and wisdom inside. I hope this book helps you to believe in your own wisdom, and listen to it.

I've also learned that people have an easier time imagining fairness in the future if they know that it existed in the past. Equality between girls and boys can't be "against nature," the way some very discouraged people say it is, because those ancient times and cultures that came before the history we usually study in school—which is why they are called "prehistory"—had much more balance between males and females. Thanks to feminist scholars and new scientific measurements that show many artifacts to be much older than experts originally thought (including some of the goddess figures you'll see in these pages), we know that, for about 95 percent of the time human beings have lived on earth, every continent had cultures in which girls were as valuable as boys, there were goddesses as well as gods, and men and women also lived in better balance with nature.

Of course, we can't go back to the past. But if everything we learn is about the last 5 percent of human history when males have been thought to be superior to females and one race has dominated another—which, I'm sorry to say, has been true for most people in the last few thousand years—then we're more likely to believe it's the natural or even the only way. As the saying goes, "If you've never seen a deer, it's hard to see a deer." If we've never seen a society in which men are equal to women as parents, or women are equal to men as leaders, it's really hard to imagine one.

When I was growing up, for instance, I remember how hard it was for girls to stand up for ourselves, and to dream about a future that didn't depend on the men we might marry. Our families, our friends, our textbooks, and just about everything in our lives seemed to be saying: *boys have always been more important—and they always will be*. Though we started out with a sense of fairness, as children do, the unfairness all around us made us feel alone, and sometimes a little crazy. (I bet there have been a lot of times when you, too, have said to yourself, "It isn't fair!") It was only after we were grown-ups that most of us began to talk to each other, discover that we were neither alone nor crazy, and start a movement for a future in which women and girls could be strong, safe, and free.

For a long time, I'd been thinking about how much it would have meant to me—and how much it could mean to girls now—if this information about ancient times were part of everyday life. The problem is that only people who were old enough to go to college learned it—providing they took women's studies or some other remedial course—or people like me, who had time to find the right books to read after college.

Then one day, I learned something from my friend Wilma Mankiller, the first woman to be elected Principal Chief of the Cherokee Nation. Her election reawakened the ancient Cherokee tradition of balance between women and men, girls and boys. I knew that, just as a council of women elders used to choose the male chief and decide when to go to war and when to make peace, Wilma's leadership symbolized a return to this balance that had been lost when the U.S. government drove the Cherokees off their land, made fun of their "petticoat government," in which treaties weren't valid unless they were signed by female leaders as well as male elders, and kept them from teaching their language in their own schools and practicing their own spiritual ceremonies—even into the 1960s. What I didn't know was that Wilma had also made a portable timeline and flash cards of Cherokee history, so it could be taken to small groups, even if they lived deep in the countryside. She said that they were helped by knowing about their past power and culture, and understanding how they had been lost—especially because they had been made to feel that they and their culture were inferior, and therefore they were at fault for their own poverty and lack of power. They gained pride in themselves, and a belief that they could help themselves.

Listening to Wilma convinced me that even a glimpse of ancient female power could help girls of all races and cultures to believe in themselves, too. Just as Wilma had taken this information around to small groups, I imagined taking it to the kind of small groups that had given birth to the women's movement—groups called consciousness-raising, rap, or support groups, where women learned from each other's experiences.

Of course, I realized that girls as young as nine or ten probably couldn't go to meetings on their own, so there would have to be women there, too. But I also knew how important those young ages were. Girls are clear-eyed and more truly themselves then, before the "feminine" role that arrives at twelve or so and creates a need to pretend. It had been my experience that girls of nine or ten not only reminded teenage girls of their true selves, but they also reminded grown-up women, too. Besides, if those grown-ups were willing to answer girls' questions honestly, that would be important, too. I remembered how much I had longed to have my questions taken seriously, and how often I still met young girls who lack the chance to learn from a variety of grown-up women who told them the truth as they had experienced it.

As I traveled around the country, I began to talk about this dream for girls and women. I talked about my hope that the inspiring knowledge of ancient history could get out of books and campuses and into everyday life. This is what organizers do: we carry ideas and encouragement from one group to another, so people don't have to keep reinventing the wheel for themselves. Still, no dream becomes a reality until it finds someone who wants to act on it—which is as it should be.

About three years before this book came out for the first time, and more than a decade ago now, when I had just about decided this particular dream wasn't meant to come true, I was speaking in a big bookstore in a small town in northern California. Andrea Johnston, the woman you are about to meet in these pages, came up afterward, and we talked more about starting such groups.

As a lifelong writer and activist on girls' and women's issues who was teaching the sixth, seventh, and eighth grades, she was one of the rare grown-ups who talked honestly with girls and was trusted by them. She had even helped several girls to speak out about a male teacher who was sexually harassing them, that is, touching and talking to them in a sexual way that made them feel uncomfortable. Andrea had become one of the first teachers in the country to support students in a case like this.

She and I met several more times to brainstorm about the kind of group that would have helped us when we were growing up, and to share what we had learned from girls about what would help them now. I realized that she could make this dream come true. After carrying the seeds around for a long time, I had found a gardener.

Over the next few months, Andrea invited diverse groups of girls and women into her home, and she tried out talks, games, artifacts, and many ways of sharing each other's wisdom. We brainstormed after each meeting about what we and the girls and women in that group thought could be better. Gradually, the news and messages of these groups began to spread and blossom, and the wind of interest spread the seeds of this dream far and wide. Groups were held in thirteen cities and towns across the country, usually during one whole day on two consecutive weekends. Each time, Andrea traveled to be the gardener. When she returned, we would brainstorm some more and think of ways to plant more gardens. Thanks to the Ms. Foundation for Women, a place where girls are a priority—for instance, the Ms. Foundation invented Take Our Daughters to Work Day®—there was a foundation that could accept contributions to Girls Speak Out before it became a nonprofit organization. Thanks to the YWCA of the USA, there were safe places for girls and women to meet nationwide. Today, there is a garden with groups growing in different countries.

I know you're wondering just what the groups are like, so you can make them your own through the pages of this book. They are a combination of what I imagined, what Andrea created from her long experience with girls, and what girls themselves have invented—and they also have a life of their own. You will experience them here in a very personal and detailed way in the pages of this book, so I will just tell you some general things. For instance:

Ages: The groups, like this book, are for girls from nine to fifteen, though that is just a guideline. As Carol Gilligan has demonstrated with her research as a psychologist at Harvard University, girls at the younger end of that spectrum still have their true voice because the feminine role hasn't descended on them yet, older ones have begun to experience those ideas of conformity, and so both tend to learn a lot from each other. Together, they "strengthen healthy rebellion," in Gilligan's phrase, and deal with such problems as the loss of freedom at twelve or so, just as boys are beginning to gain freedom.

The presence of women not only may offer a girl her first chance to ask an older woman questions, but it may also teach her that questioning is part of every stage of life, and that grown-up women don't have all the answers either. For women, listening to girls' true voices often reawakens the rebellious girl within, helps them to realize the price paid when that little girl was "shushed," and shows them that she needn't be silenced anymore. Women also become more aware of the danger of silencing girls in the present.

Andrea also discovered that young women in their late teens or early twenties could play a special role. They represent the next stage of life for nine- to fifteen-year-olds, yet are close enough in age and experience to have great credibility. Two or three women in their late teens and twenties often serve as facilitators.

Diversity: Just as a variety of ages offer more chances for each girl to expand her world, so do different races, classes, lifestyles, and abilities. That had been my experience as an organizer, and Andrea's as a teacher, so from the beginning, each group has included different races, economic groups, and backgrounds—from girls who live in housing projects to girls who board at private schools, from girls who speak two languages to girls whose real language is drawing or music. Near the beginning of the first day, Andrea sometimes asks a question: "What is different about us—and what is the same?" Or: "Go up to the girl who seems most different from you, and ask the question you're most afraid to ask." Usually, girls discover how many identities each girl has, and how hard it is to tell what's inside from what's outside.

Talking about goddesses and ancient history from every culture and part of the world also leads to understanding diversity. At a session I attended in New York, for instance, Andrea shaped seven big pieces of colored cloth like the seven continents, put them on the floor, and asked each girl to stand on the one she identified with—either because her family came from there, or because she just felt drawn to it. In that setting, we all knew that, if there was a continent without a girl on it, the world was not complete.

Using All Five Senses: Since I am an inside-my-head kind of person, I had to learn from Andrea the importance of starting out with physical games that everyone can do, for instance, a simple game of clapping in different rhythms. When diverse girls do one thing together, they feel more like a group. If each of us uses our whole body, we also feel more whole. While you're reading this book, for example, you might do something physical every once in a while, like dancing or some exercise. There is no separation between our minds and our bodies. We all learn better when all five senses are alert.

Instead of just reading about ancient goddesses from all different cultures, for instance, we found replicas that girls can touch, pass around, and make up stories about, seeing how images of female power make them feel—just as girls in ancient times did. The girls also do lots of hands-on, all-five-senses things, like using clay, paints, and markers, keeping journals—just about every form of expression.

My favorite activity is using our voices to read aloud and tell stories. After all, stories and narratives have been used to teach for thousands of years. They take us on a journey instead of presenting us with its conclusion, they let us imagine ourselves in someone else's shoes, and they make it clear that no situation is quite like any other. At the end of the first day, for instance, we always read *Finding the Green Stone* by Alice Walker, a story that inspired us to find many more. We also give each girl a green stone to symbolize her true self.

After all, we have to be truthful about how hard life is sometimes. But we also need to know there is a special place inside each of us where no one else can go. A place we can hold onto, like the green stone. A place that is a unique combination of billions of years of heredity and environment that has come together in each of us in a unique way that could never have happened before and could never happen again. That is where our unique voice comes from.

If Andrea and I have learned anything over these years, it's how unique each girl is, and how much she affects and is affected by everyone around her. I think that's the secret we want to share with you: We are independent and interdependent. Each of us is unique, and needs a community that supports that uniqueness.

I hope these groups will be the beginning of a national, grassroots movement that belongs to girls, a whole country blooming with young voices and faces that have never been heard or seen before. Spirits of the past will also be helping these groups, from Cherokee girls and others from the hundreds of tribes that once roamed freely on this same land, to your mothers and grandmothers who met in suffragist and abolitionist, civil rights and feminist groups to recover their freedom.

As Rayna Green, a modern Cherokee writer and anthropologist, wrote, "A feminist revolution here would simply honor American tradition, not overthrow it." Indeed, people from other continents put it even more simply, "Feminism is memory."

This book you hold in your hands is a new way of spreading seeds. But what happens must be what *you* want to happen. Its seeds and example will help others to bloom, too. What blooms in you will be your true self. Now, you are the gardener and the flower.

—Gloria Steinem

Introduction

It has been nearly a decade since I wrote this book, and in that time more people have worked to change society and make it fair to you. There are more books, magazines, newsletters, products, and events for girls. There are websites, CDs, DVDs, and video games. There are more programs focusing on girls' self-esteem as well as classes to raise math, science, and basketball scores. It's exciting to know more people are thinking about you and trying to make your life better.

The best news is, more of you are finding your true selves and each other. After all, the Girls' Movement is about girls changing things *for themselves*. It's about *being in charge*. It will take time to make life better for all girls, but day by day, girls are making a difference; girls of different races, classes, cultures, sexual orientations, and abilities are finding ways to be themselves and also to be part of a larger movement.

But a movement starts with individuals like you. This introduction will let you know what other girls have done and are doing to make girls feel more powerful and to inspire them to challenge what's unfair. It may help you hold onto who you are as you grow up. Most of it comes from girls themselves on five continents who write to me and share their connection with the ideas and people in this book. It's important to know there are girls like you, especially if you don't know girls with similar interests in your community.

When I travel, I talk with girls in different countries, and when I'm at home, I correspond with girls all over the world. No matter where they are, one of the things I share with them is what researchers have discovered often happens to girls growing up in male-dominated societies, which is happening in every country today. Many of these researchers are women working in universities who interview and observe groups of girls over time. Even though most studies focus on white girls from middle-class families, girls of color and girls from other economic classes tell me the same things happen to them—but in different ways. Similar studies of more diverse groups of girls are also being conducted now in many countries. In the meantime, you can decide for yourself whether the findings are true for you and girls you know.

Here is what can happen: Most girls silence themselves between the ages of nine and sixteen; that is, they give up a part of who they are because they think it's necessary to do so to survive. They begin to act like a stereotype, a false idea of what it means to be female. Girls play the more feminine role that is based on the mistaken belief that females are weaker than males. There is a lot of pressure on girls to fit this stereotype rather than fight for their unique differences. For example, girls want to be thin, even anorexic or bulimic, because girls of different sizes and shapes are not as easily accepted. Carol Gilligan, one of the first researchers to study girls, describes the change in many girls as losing their different and unique voices. Instead of trusting themselves, girls may become uncertain and lose self-confidence.

How do you feel about these discoveries? Girls who are nine years old and haven't reached this point yet usually say, "No way. It's not going to happen to me." Girls who are fifteen and sixteen often shake their heads and say, "Yes, it's happening" or "It's already happened." Wherever I go, and in the letters and emails I receive, girls who have lost their voice describe what happened to them and say they don't want it to happen to other girls. Some say people tease them if they say positive things about girls and women. Many girls stop raising their hand in class because they've decided it's safer being ignored than drawing attention to themselves by knowing the answer. Girls who are treated as objects, some of whom are seriously abused, pretend everything is okay. They feel powerless, and they don't know what else to do.

While it's important to know that some girls lose their voice, research also shows that girls are *resilient*, which means they have the ability to bounce back when something unfair happens. So the lesson is, even if you lose your voice, you can get it back.

Being aware of what often happens to girls can help girls hold onto their voice. For example, Lakesha, a seven-year-old girl from Houston, Texas, went with her parents to a bookstore where I was speaking and signing copies of *Girls Speak Out*. She was sitting on the floor near me, waiting for her parents. Soon she stopped drawing on the napkin she had on her lap and stared at me for a long time. I asked her what she wanted to say. Here is part of our conversation:

"'Sexism,' 'sexism.' You keep saying 'sexism.' What does it mean?"

"It's what's outside you that says boys and men are better than girls and women," I answered. "It's supposed to be true whether or not it feels right."

"Oh," said Lakesha, "I didn't know it had a name."

Lakesha asked people at the book signing to share ideas on how to "change the rules at school that say I can't play on the football team even though I like football."

Sometimes people don't take even older girls seriously because of a mistaken belief that girls can't do things on their own.

A girl in North Carolina wrote to me about her solution to a problem: "I tried to start a group for girls in my area. Although there were loads of wonderful women willing to help, I got little response from schools. I think it was hard for them to believe a sixteen-year-old girl like me was serious about bringing girls in her community together." However, she said, "I intend to work on this project again when I graduate. I'll have more time than I do now to visit each school I want to involve and to write articles for the newspaper."

Lots of girls find it's exciting to be among the first in the Girls' Movement. It's also a challenge. Sometimes it can be lonely if people around you have different ideas. Amulya and I have been emailing each other since she began high school four years ago. After she read this book, she wanted to organize girls in her school in India and find out their opinions. She began doing surveys, and at first she was frustrated and angry: "I wish I felt as energetic as you are thinking I am. I am all out. I have been feeling so low the past few days. I feel I'm getting into one of those stereotypic images of girls that I have always hated. I don't know why.

"My school is supposed to be a school that encourages and sets new trends, and the girls are supposed to be really confident and all that. But the truth is many of them are idiots. They still believe that girls should be submissive etc. They all want to get married and 'settle down.' They are not worried about freedom and careers, and sometimes when I do something outspoken about girls' rights, they say it's gross and girls are not supposed to do that etc. It's all so irritating. And what's worse, I sometimes have to agree with them." Can you identify with Amulya's mood? Sometimes I also feel like too few people care about girls. But this mood passes because people who are starting something new, especially close to home, know it's hard work as well as fun.

Here's what Amulya wrote in a recent email: "People say that colours reflect your mood. I'm on a high right now like bright red and yellow or a deep purple. I finished my tests and now we have fests, loads of them, and they are really fun. This time we're coming up with new ideas, and I am on creative teams to have events about choices for girls' futures, and it's rocking. It's busy, but it's fun. At the end of the day when I think about how many things I have done, I wonder how I managed to find time to do all those things and still I don't feel tired. I love arranging things to let people know girls are strong, and people say I am good at it. I come up with crazy ideas that others and I feel are good. And that's what counts for an activist like me."

When I tell girls about girls in other places, like Amulya and Lakesha, they often want to meet each other. When I first began the program, girls in different parts of the USA who participated in Girls Speak Out programs wanted to have a global girls' conference. The National (USA) Girls Coalition was formed in 1995 to help organize it. It became a model for other girls' conferences, and it is something you can adapt for your own community.

The most important thing we did was to trust girls and give them control over the content of the conference. We also eliminated an adult keynote speaker so girls could see each other as role models, have more time to meet each other, become friends, and create their own Plan of Action. Women were on a panel talking about their girlhoods, and others volunteered to take notes during workshops.

From the beginning, girls helped to plan the First National Girls' Conference. Girls from four different regions of the USA formed a Girls Steering Committee that met monthly. The steering committee chose topics that women had discussed at the Fourth World Conference on Women, which was sponsored by the United Nations and took place in Beijing in 1995. Those topics were Confronting Violence against Girls, Girls' Rights, and Images of Girls in the Media.

We wanted to hold the conference at the United Nations headquarters in New York City, but it was unusual for girls to organize an event there. At a meeting of the National Girls' Coalition, girls asked a woman representing the United Nations if there could be a sleepover at the United Nations during the conference. She explained that it had never been done before; it would be difficult, if not impossible, to arrange. Clara, an eleven-year-old member of the Girls Steering Committee, was sitting across the big oval table from the United Nations representative. Clara pulled her chair closer to the table and leaned toward the woman.

"I know what the problem is," Clara said. "When the United Nations was built, you didn't think about girls. That's okay. We can still work it out."

There was a moment of silence. Then the woman smiled at Clara and said, "Maybe if we had thought about you, and sleepovers, there wouldn't be so many wars and fights."

The conference was held on January 3 and 4, 1997. More than 140 girls from thirty-nine states attended along with girls from eleven countries including the USA. They were of different races, classes, cultures, sexual orientations, and abilities. They lived at home, at school, in shelters, or in group homes. The National Girls' Coalition had raised money to pay each girl's travel and living expenses. The United States Committee for UNICEF (which stands for the United Nations International Children's Fund) is the organization that cosponsored the conference. It brought the girls from various countries in Africa, Asia, Latin America, and Europe. We met at UNICEF House in New York City, right across the street from the United Nations.

Girls at the conference were as unique as each of you reading this book. They were eight to sixteen years old. They included a fifteen-year-old girl who lived on a fishing boat in Alaska; girls aged nine to sixteen from public housing developments in New York, Chicago, and New Jersey; an eleven-year-old from a ski resort in Montana; a ten-year-old who lived on Central Park West in New York City; a nine-year-old from a Native American reservation in Minnesota; and two sisters from a village on the Ivory Coast.

It was magical when all these different girls came together. Soon they were one clear, powerful voice. For two days, girls worked to create a Girls Global Plan of Action that is used as a model in many countries. They wanted a document that showed what girls think and how they could change things. You can find part of it at the end of this book, and you can send for more information about the Girls Global Plan of Action using the contact information listed at the end of this introduction. Although the girls worked hard, they also told jokes and sang.

Two girls who have worked with Girls Speak Out since it began, and also helped organize the conference, want to tell you about their experience before and at the girls' conference. Christina Dry writes about events leading up to the conference:

Hi! I was a girl from a small town in northern California when I helped start Girls Speak Out. My mother is Japanese-American, and she grew up in Hawaii. My father is white, and he spent most of his life in Monte Rio, which is where my older sister, Cindy, and I grew up, too.

I'd managed, sometimes unintentionally, to go against almost every stereotype set for girls, especially Asian girls. I'm outspoken about anything and everything. I've loved playing sports all my life. I've played basketball and softball forever, and in school I was on the varsity teams for basketball, softball, running, and swimming. I participated in sports that make you sweat, which I was told is very unladylike. But you know what? I don't care! I never worried about all the frills girls are supposed to worry about.

I helped create Girls Speak Out almost ten years ago. It started with meetings in Andrea's classroom when I was eleven and she was my sixth-grade teacher. Soon the girls and I moved from talking about our personal problems to problems other girls experience.

I remember being in Andrea's living room for one of our first meetings after she left teaching. There were about eight or nine girls, and we were all sitting in a circle on the floor. Andrea had a ceramic box that was cut and painted to look like a thick book with a pumpkin on the cover. It was called Cinderella 1990 *(by Constance Alyce Westvig Roberts). Inside the box were about fifteen miniature wooden feet and one wooden slipper. The feet were different sizes and colors. Some had dainty, painted toenails and others were hairy. Some stood out more than others did, but none of them fit the little wooden slipper.*

We sat there in a circle comparing the different feet when we suddenly made a connection between them and ourselves. The feet were symbolic of all of us. Some of us were big and others were little. We were different colors and from different backgrounds. The little wooden slipper represented the stereotypes and borders that have been set for girls. None of the feet fit the slipper, just as most girls don't fit stereotypes set for us.

Girls shouldn't fit stereotypes because stereotypes are so unrealistic. Knowing this has made a huge impact on the way I live my life. Life becomes much simpler and more enjoyable when you don't worry about being someone you're not.

I believe the most important part of Girls Speak Out is diversity. Girls from different places, races, cultures, and classes bring different views and experiences into the discussions. Sometimes I feel as if my personal experiences are very different from most girls. As I learn about more girls' lives, I understand how our different experiences make us more interesting and my world bigger. For example, I was a member of the Girls Steering Committee for the First National Girls' Conference. I worked to organize the conference with girls in Minnesota, West Virginia, and New York City.

We were discussing topics to cover at the conference. Each girl could choose three from a list of fifteen topics. The girls in New York wanted to include Violence against Girls. I didn't see the importance of it because violence isn't a big part of my life. As we talked, I realized what it is like for girls who live with violence every day. Now I know it's the number one problem in girls' lives around the world.

Experiences like these have formed a new understanding for me of how the world works. They make me feel good about myself. I've done something to change things. All these experiences helped me realize how much I can get done, and how much any girl can do.

I thought of the slogan we used at the conference, "Don't Deal with It! Change It!" I guess that's what I've been doing and what I will do all my life.

Elizabeth "Lizard" Foster-Shaner has been working in the Girls' Movement since she was nine years old. She started by writing speeches and organizing plays about girls and women when she was in middle school. She's an actor and a writer. Lizard was fifteen at the time of the conference. She recently graduated from the

University of California at Berkeley, and she creates and organizes street theatre productions.

Each girl who came and participated in the conference sent in an application. We were assured each girl was serious in her beliefs and desire for change. Women mentors were there to take notes and to help the girls, but only if we asked them. After all, it was our conference. We saw artifacts from prehistory that show us how girls and women were important. Sharing what we felt helped us feel each girl's power.

Next, we broke into groups. Each workshop had about fifteen to twenty girls, and three steering committee girls were the leaders. Each girl went to three workshops, one on each topic: Confronting Violence against Girls, Girls' Rights, and Images of Girls in the Media. We listed how the topics affect us and brainstormed a plan of action. Some of our ideas were to start a girls' group at home or at school, write a girls' newsletter, and start a web page and chat room as a girls' support center.

We focused on talking about our personal experiences. We used statistics. There were many problems talked about at the conference from our right to be ourselves to safely walking the streets at night. Our goal at the conference was to find some answers to these problems. After each girl had participated in one workshop on each theme, we gathered one last time at a speak-out to come up with our plan of action. So many ideas! They included support groups for victims of abuse as young as four and five years old, sending our plan to governors and the president, and having mini-conferences at home.

The conference was not only the official start of the Girls' Movement. I think it was also a chance for girls to find hope and meet other girls with the same feelings and thoughts.

There has never been such a sharing of ideas and feelings. I am very proud I was part of it. It helped me believe that no matter what, we are going to make the future ours.

If you want to share what you're doing in the Girls' Movement, you can write to the Girls Speak Out Action Network at the address at the end of this introduction. Remember, there are as many ways to be active as there are girls. You don't have to participate in a conference to help make a bright future. What you do and say matters, whether you stay close to home or connect with people in different states and countries.

Two years ago, I went to the YWCA Toronto, Canada, for a Girls Speak Out workshop. I hoped to find a woman who could train other women to help spread the program without me in charge. I found a young woman named Amy, and a few months ago, with the help of other women at the YWCA Toronto, she began training women from the YWCA of Canada. Today, we are certifying Girls Speak Out workshop leaders all over Canada. A group of young women in Fiji are also working with me to train organizers and bring the program to females in schools all over the islands.

I never imagined that so many girls and women outside my native country, the USA, would respond so deeply to this book and to the Girls Speak Out program. One of my latest dreams is to have girl-led program workshops just as the First National Girls' Conference was girl-led. I believe it will happen in the next decade because I see, hear, and feel girls growing stronger no matter where they live.

For now, women's help is essential to ensure that girls connect with each other and raise powerful voices across oceans and continents. Wherever they are, women know that girls are strong and brave. I hope this book helps you imagine and live in a new millennium in which girls everywhere will be inspired to be their true selves all their lives.

Over time, I've developed a trusted network in the United Nations and with nonprofit organizations in different parts of the world that support girls who speak out in a way they choose. There is someone near you who will reach out to you if and when you ask or need help and/or inspiration. For more information, to ask questions, to give answers, and to share your ideas, plans, and experiences, please use the following:

Girls Speak Out Action Network
c/o Ten Speed Press
PO Box 7123
Berkeley, CA 94707
USA
www.girlsspeakout.org
Email: GspeakOut@aol.com

Remember, Don't Deal with It! Change It!

OPENINGS

We believe everyone
matters. —*Andrea*

I'm sitting by myself writing to you, and you are probably sitting by yourself reading, yet we're not alone. We're connected by the words in this book. Words are a way of touching each other when we are not in the same room—or living during the same time.

When I was growing up, I used to run away into books. Sometimes I was lonely and felt as if I wasn't connected to anyone around me. Sometimes I was escaping from something bad that was happening. I wanted to enter a world where I could fly over the city and be whoever I wanted to be.

I knew I could do whatever I wanted to do, even if I was a girl, because there were strong females in the stories I read. I invented my own stories, too, in which girls were leaders, but people told me girls were supposed to just watch and help out because we couldn't do a lot of the best stuff. Now I know they are wrong about us. We can do whatever we want to do. We just need to learn how powerful we are and be reminded that powerful women once were commonplace.

When I was ten years old, I ran away from home because I thought I wouldn't be allowed to be who I was. I had a new baby brother whom everyone thought was special simply because he was a boy, and after having two daughters my parents "finally had a son." The adults around me were being *sexist*, that is, they were judging us by our sex and deciding boys were better than girls. I love my brother, but I didn't like feeling that I was a disappointment because I was born a girl, so I left a note for my parents hidden inside one of my favorite books, an illustrated copy of *Alice in Wonderland.* They never found the note, of course, and I came back before they missed me, hungry for lunch. Like Alice, I learned that my world can turn upside down and that it's important to check inside for direction, too. Today, books are still a place where I can find messages that help me stay true to myself. Books are like coming home for me.

Check Ins

From time to time in these pages you will find a special connecting place called a Check In. You'll be asked to write, draw, paint, do, or think about something you have read. It's a good idea to have a notebook nearby in which you can record your reactions. You could also collect some blank or almost empty pages and bend the corners to keep them together like a notebook.

You can choose whether or not to follow the suggestions in a Check In. You are in control no matter how old you are. I hope you discover that a Check In helps you to express the valuable ideas, plans, and dreams you have inside you. Girls and women of all ages from different parts of the world will share their true selves with you in these pages. Check Ins can help bring you into a circle with them. Your notebook is a place you can return to again and again and be free to explore your inner world no matter what is happening around you.

Books have messages in them; that is, we learn how an author feels about something, and we can apply it to our own lives. What messages about being a girl have you found in books? What do you do when you disagree with ideas about girls that you find in books? Which message about girls would you like to find in a book and share with other people? Write your message about girls on a long, narrow piece of paper that is shaped like a bumper sticker to remind you and/or let others know what you think about being a girl. What you write is important, too.

Our True Self

Now I'm grown-up. Even my son, Jesse, has grown up. But I'm living my life with books as a writer working with girls, and I continue to look for messages in books. So you see, sometimes the things we love when we are very young can help to remind us who we are no matter how old we are. Our true self never changes. Like a seed that grows into one particular flower, the wisdom is always inside.

In the last ten years, I've found a new way to connect girls, books, and women, just as I wished I could have been connected when I was growing up. A friend, Gloria, and I created a special program for young girls that grew into this book. As we developed the program, we learned that we can walk into a room of girls and women we don't know, and before the day is over, we've all become friends who trust and help each other. Have you ever had an experience like this?

Gloria and I are feminists. That means we believe *everyone matters*: for instance, that girls are as important as boys, that no one race or religion is more important than another, and that all people can make decisions for themselves. "Feminism" is a word that includes everyone. I think of it as an "and" word, meaning girls *and* boys and black *and* white women instead of meaning girls *or* boys and black *or* white women.

The problem is that girls aren't treated as equals to boys. To some degree, in all countries in the world, males are treated better than females because of an old and wrong belief that males are superior. That's why girls need to know that they're strong, that the unfair system we live in is the problem. In other words, girls are okay, but a lot of the system isn't. Girls of color usually know this at an earlier age than white girls because judging people by their skin color has been as much a problem as judging people by whether they're male or female for about five thousand years. Now, it is at least recognized as wrong to be prejudiced about race, but too few people understand that sexism is a prejudice, too.

Girls Speak Out Program

Gloria and I created a special program for girls nine to fifteen years old because that's the important changeover time from being a child to being a grown-up. In the last decade, girls aged sixteen to twenty have come to these programs or read about them because they want to be sure to have positive information about being a girl, too. A few older girls and women also attend. They are asked to focus on sharing their experiences of growing up so girls can see

Many People Can Be Wrong

How do you feel about the idea that girls are okay and boys are not better than girls? What two arguments would you use to show that girls are just as powerful as boys? For instance, "Girls can do as well as boys in math and science," "Girls can play sports like soccer and basketball," or "Girls can become heads of government."

Whom do you trust enough to share your ideas with about girls as powerful people? Some of you may feel safe when you express a belief in girls' power, but some of you live where expressing such beliefs is dangerous. Even though each of us has a right to express our true beliefs and feelings, girls who feel unsafe have to be extra careful.

Think about when and how you could talk with a trusted friend in safety. Hopefully, your trusted friend will help you find a place where you can freely share your ideas about powerful females, even if they're not the ideas you are expected to have. Your ideas and feelings are important no matter where you are, no matter what others think about them, and no matter how old you are. As a matter of fact, many people believe that what happens when you're a girl is at least as important as what will happen to you when you're a woman. Your impressions of family life and the importance of an education, for example, are formed when you're very young. They're a foundation that you build on, and don't replace, as you age. What qualities or parts of your personality and character that you have now do you want to hold onto as you grow up?

many different kinds of experiences and have their questions answered. The program and this book are both called Girls Speak Out because they have the same purpose, which is to help girls stay strong and to believe in their true selves. Together, the program and book reach many girls and show many people how powerful girls really are.

The program is divided into two workshops that are usually held a week apart to give girls a chance to think about and react to what happens in the first workshop. We talk, listen to stories, play games, eat, and have fun over two days together. You will have a chance to share many of these same things while reading this book, but you decide how much time to spend with each activity.

Girls Speak Out explores the past as well as the future of females. You will learn about a time long ago, before the history you probably learn in school, when females were as powerful and honored as males, and even the gods were often women. This was true all over the earth no matter where girls and women lived. I collect information like this to help girls learn that the way things are now is not the way things always were, or the way they always have to be in the future. No matter what, girls, women, and their friends are going to help create a world in which each individual girl is powerful. In this world, boys would also be free to be who *they* really are. But it helps a lot to know that things were not always the way they are now, and there was once a time when females were honored—and so was nature and all living things.

As I mentioned before, you can experience Girls Speak Out in different ways. Girls have told me that when they were reading these pages they felt connected to their own deep feelings and to those of the people in this book. They have many of the same experiences described by girls in the workshops. Both readers and workshop participants tell me they've learned that they can find the strength, courage, and support inside themselves and in other girls and women to help them succeed. One way of being part of Girls Speak Out isn't better than another way.

Check In A Girls Speak Out Collection

The girls you will meet in this book are different ages, they look different from each other, and they come from different countries and continents. You can create your own picture collection of the girls and women you might meet in a Girls Speak Out program by cutting out photos and illustrations from newspapers, magazines, drawings, paintings, postcards, or catalogues. Find pictures that show thin girls, girls with different shades of skin color, fat girls, girls with big or tiny breasts, girls with long and short hair, girls working with tools, and girls in school or working in the fields. Women can be shown doing some if not all of the same things. After all, the world is filled with females who look different from each other. What name will you give to your book of pictures of girls? As you read, I will ask you to refer back to your collection. You can also share your Girls Speak Out picture collection with someone you trust as a way to spread the word about the amazing diversity among girls.

I hope these pages are a place for you to find and hold onto your true self. You can hear your own voice whether or not you use Check Ins because each chapter contains voices of girls like you who believe in their true selves and of women who remain true to themselves even after they've grown up.

Girl power doesn't have borders as countries do. Girl power is everywhere. For instance, fifteen-year-old Amulya emailed this message from India: "Girls must learn how powerful they are, and I will be there to show them now and when I'm a woman." Rebecca in the northeastern United States told me, "I have just started organizing a Girls Speak Out club, and what I am doing has changed some of the people who don't understand that girls have the same power as boys." Despite the distance between them, Amulya and Rebecca believe girls are important and strong. There are no natural or national boundaries among girls.

Girls say it's often difficult to find a place to get together and meet. Eleven-year-old Katie who lives in Australia said, "I don't own a living room. My parents do. We get along, but I don't know how my mother will react if girls show up one morning." Katie decided that meeting with her two closest friends in a park for lunch and talking about the ideas and people in this book was what she really wanted to do. Her mother was happy to transport them and sit nearby to visit with a friend.

If you want to bring girls and women together in person as well as in pictures, you will find a section with information on participating in Girls Speak Out workshops at the end of this book. Girls say that it's important to have at least one supportive woman to act as a helper for regular meetings and workshops. You can decide whether you want to help organize or lead an actual Girls Speak Out program for as few as two or as many as twenty girls and women.

Reading this book may be all you want to do, and that's fine, too. Whether you attend a program or read this book or do both of these things, this book is a place you can visit whenever you want, like a memory. You can choose how to use it now and as you're growing up. It can change as you do because your reactions to what you read in these pages and how you respond to Check Ins will change as you age. This book belongs to you no matter how old you are.

Naming Ourselves

Girls have the right to
understand their
importance in society.
—*Maya*

I hope you have a comfortable place to sit or stretch out as you read this book. Making ourselves comfortable is important in a workshop, too, even if it means moving furniture. Perhaps you have a favorite spot to read that's outside on the grass or maybe you'd rather be inside in a quiet corner away from a noisy street. Some of you might have a few pillows to snuggle with as you read through these pages. Girls often bring pillows to a workshop, and we make room for them to stretch out or curl up. You decide when you're cozy. You're part of Girls Speak Out whether you are reading these pages by yourself or in a workshop.

The thoughts and feelings of girls who have read this book and who have participated in workshops are captured here for you to share. The variety of girls in your picture collection looks like girls who read this book and like girls in the workshops. We've

What's Up with Your Name?

One of the first things we do in workshops is to make name tags. Girls and women usually pin name tags on their shirts; some girls will put them on their pants, and one girl in New Jersey stuck hers on upside-down so she could read it and look at the stars she decorated her name with.

Now is a good time to get your notebook or pieces of paper that you can write or draw on. That way, you'll be going through the same steps as you would if we were in the same room. When you're ready, write your name as you want it to look. Draw a shape and put your name inside it. It can be straight or curved or look like a puddle. My name tag says "Andrea" in green because it's a special color for me. What color would you choose for your name? Would you use more than one color? One color for each letter? Do you make tiny circles or a heart over the letter *i*? Your name is an important part of you. Maybe you have chosen a special name for yourself; if so, that's the name we would read on your name tag. If you make a name tag, you can wear it or use it as a bookmark or do whatever you want with it.

After all, it's your name tag.

found that the more kinds of experiences there are, the more everybody has to learn from, and we deliberately include girls from as many different backgrounds as possible.

Katie (Australia), Amulya (India), and Rebecca (USA), about whom you've already heard, never attended a Girls Speak Out program in person. They read this book just like you're doing now and wrote to me online or by snail mail. They live thousands of miles from each other, yet their feelings about being a girl are so close to being the same that it's as if they grew up next door to each other. From the inside out, girls like you are filled with possibilities for connection.

If you have a friend who's also reading *Girls Speak Out*, you can write or draw messages to each other on certain pages or in a special section in your notebook. If you are reading alone, you can talk to your notebook as if it's a diary or a journal. If you decide you want to show your notebook to someone, you choose the time to share it. And since I love being a reader, you are welcome to send your writings or drawings to me at the address in the introduction to this book. There are many ways to share and many people with whom you can share. Again, it's your choice.

Name Tag Game

Name tags are important because you can use them in a game that girls can play before they sit down and get to know each other. The game we play with name tags in the workshop introduces us to each other. Imagine playing the name tag game with your friends; you can be the leader. Here's what a twenty-three-year-old woman named Anastasia taught us:

- All the girls and women stand in a circle. There are usually as many females in the circle as we have fingers and toes, about twenty of us all together, counting you and me. If it's any more than that, there isn't enough time for each person to be heard and for everybody to learn from each other.
- We make certain we can see each person's name tag.
- Then we go around the circle and say our names out loud so we can hear how to say them. Some girls have unusual

names, like Wislene or Casha. You'll see a lot of girls' names throughout these pages. You may want to say them out loud. Would your name be easy or challenging to pronounce?

- If two people have the same name, we figure out what to call each person. In West Virginia, where a girl and a woman both had the name Kathryn, the girl wanted to be called Kat, and the woman stayed with Kathryn.

- Once we hear and practice saying each other's names, we're ready to move forward. It's important to call each person what she likes to be called so we practice doing these things right away.

- Someone, usually me, who knows the game, or you—because you're reading this and now you'll know it, too—goes first by clapping her hands and saying someone else's name out loud. When we clap, we point our hands at the girl whose name we're saying. Then it's her turn to clap at another girl and say her name.

- The game continues like this until we build up speed, and it sounds like we're all clapping together. Or sometimes some girls and women will try different clapping rhythms.

In New York City, fifteen-year-old Tiffany decided to stand in the center of the circle and close her eyes. Then she clapped each person's name from memory as she turned around inside the circle. I think changing the rules is fun because it makes the game belong to you. The Girls Speak Out name tag game is invented again and again so it's always original, like you.

After playing this game and/or reading about it, it may be time to take a snack break. Do you take snack breaks while you're reading? I usually start reading with an apple or an orange next to me. It's okay to eat and drink during the workshops, too—it makes us feel more comfortable if we know we can eat when we're hungry. I hope you are allowed to eat while you read if you like to. Even when I was teaching in public school, students in my room could eat healthy snacks during reading time.

Taking time to honor your name, and the unique person it represents, is a powerful way to begin a journey like the one we're on together.

Being Eleven

I'm happy when I help
someone learn that girls
are strong. —*Rachel*

A name is something people learn about us, but our first impression of each other often comes from simply looking at each other. Sometimes when people look at us, they just see our bodies, not who we really are inside. And sometimes certain people decide they want to stay away from us because we look a particular way, and those people have been told that the way we look, which is different than the way they look, is bad. This is a problem with the people who are looking at us, not with us.

One of these problems is called *racism*. Racism happens when people are judged by their race or skin color. Actually, skin color is determined by how much of a chemical called melanin we have in our skin. The more melanin, the darker the skin.

Another problem is called *classism*. Classism happens when people are judged by how much money they have, by how poor or rich they are, or by their family's class or ranking in the community.

Sexism occurs when people are judged by their gender, which is whether they're male or female.

Ageism, when people are judged based on their age, can be a problem, too, because people are often convinced that children have to grow up before their words and feelings are valuable.

You can see how silly these isms are by inventing your own ism. For instance, *chinism*, if there were such a thing, would be a way of judging someone by how much bone and flesh is on her or his chin.

While sexism may appear to be the most important problem in a book like this for girls, the truth is that girls are unfairly judged in a lot of ways. Brainstorm as many words as you can that describe your experience with sexism, racism, ageism, or classism. Write a poem using some or all of the words that express your feelings. Have you talked about these experiences with someone? If you have, write about how it feels to share an unhappy experience. If you haven't, please describe what you want to have happen when you do share a painful experience. If you feel comfortable, ask your parent(s) if they experienced any of the isms as a child. How did they feel? Do they have any advice for you? Does their advice seem helpful or not? What advice would you have for a girl who was hurt by a sexist, racist, or classist person?

Stories

Reading stories is an important part of Girls Speak Out. It's something we can share whether we are reading silently, reading aloud, or listening. In this book, when you see words written in italics, *like this*, it means you'll be reading a story. One of the special things about reading this book is that I was able to include more stories than we can listen to in a workshop. I usually choose stories depending on who's in the room; for example, if the girls talk a lot about their mothers, I'll read a story about mothers and daughters and skip another kind of story. Here, you choose to flip through the pages and read the stories, or you can read each one as it appears. You can choose your favorites from the broad selection in this book, and you can also make up your own stories to write in your notebook.

After I read the first story aloud in a workshop, girls take turns reading and I listen. Listening to a reader links us with another voice just as hearing your inner voice links you to the words on this page. You, too, can read aloud from the story excerpts throughout this book.

Our first story is a short story written by one of my favorite writers, Sandra Cisneros. She's Mexican-American and she grew up in Chicago, a city with many neighborhoods where people of different colors and cultures live. Sandra writes about a girl in a big city who is unfairly treated by an ageist teacher in this story, "Eleven," from Cisneros' book *Woman Hollering Creek and Other Stories*.

> *What they don't understand about birthdays and what they never tell you is that when you're eleven, you're also ten, and nine, and eight, and seven, and six, and five, and four, and three, and two, and one. And when you wake up on your eleventh birthday you*

expect to feel eleven, but you don't. You open your eyes and everything's just like yesterday, only it's today. And you don't feel eleven at all. You feel like you're still ten. And you are—underneath the year that makes you eleven.

Like some days you might say something stupid, and that's the part of you that's still ten. Or maybe some days you might need to sit on your mama's lap because you're scared, and that's the part of you that's five. And maybe one day when you're all grown up maybe you will need to cry like if you're three, and that's okay. That's what I tell Mama when she's sad and needs to cry. Maybe she's feeling three.

Because the way you grow old is kind of like an onion or like the rings inside a tree trunk or like my little wooden dolls that fit one inside the other, each year inside the next one. That's how being eleven years old is.

You don't feel eleven. Not right away. It takes a few days, weeks even, sometimes months before you say Eleven when they ask you. And you don't feel smart eleven, not until you're almost twelve. That's the way it is.

Only today I wish I didn't have only eleven years rattling inside me like pennies in a tin Band-Aid box. Today I wish I was one hundred and two instead of eleven because if I was one hundred and two I'd have known what to say when Mrs. Price put the red sweater on my desk. I would've known how to tell her it wasn't mine instead of just sitting there with that look on my face and nothing coming out of my mouth.

"Whose is this?" Mrs. Price says, and she holds the red sweater up in the air for all the class to see. "Whose? It's been sitting in the coatroom for a month."

"Not mine," says everybody. "Not me."

"It has to belong to somebody," Mrs. Price keeps saying, but nobody can remember. It's an ugly sweater with red plastic buttons

and a collar and sleeves all stretched out like you could use it for a jump rope. It's maybe a thousand years old and even if it belonged to me I wouldn't say so.

Maybe because I'm skinny, maybe because she doesn't like me, that stupid Sylvia Saldivar says, "I think it belongs to Rachel." An ugly sweater like that, all raggedy and old, but Mrs. Price believes her. Mrs. Price takes the sweater and puts it right on my desk, but when I open my mouth nothing comes out.

"That's not, I don't, you're not . . . Not mine," I finally say in a little voice that was maybe me when I was four.

"Of course it's yours," Mrs. Price says. "I remember you wearing it once." Because she's older and the teacher, she's right and I'm not.

Not mine, not mine, not mine, but Mrs. Price is already turning to page thirty-two, and math problem number four. I don't know why but all of a sudden I'm feeling sick inside, like the part of me that's three wants to come out of my eyes, only I squeeze them shut tight and bite down on my teeth real hard and try to remember today I am eleven, eleven. Mama is making a cake for me tonight, and when Papa comes home everybody will sing Happy birthday, happy birthday to you.

But when the sick feeling goes away and I open my eyes, the red sweater's still sitting there like a big red mountain. I move the red sweater to the corner of my desk with my ruler. I move my pencil and books and eraser as far from it as possible. I even move my chair a little to the right. Not mine, not mine, not mine.

In my head I'm thinking how long till lunchtime, how long till I can take the red sweater and throw it over the schoolyard fence, or leave it hanging on a parking meter, or bunch it up into a little ball and toss it in the alley. Except when math period ends Mrs. Price says loud and in front of everybody, "Now, Rachel, that's enough," because she sees I've shoved the red sweater to the tippy-

tip corner of my desk and it's hanging all over the edge like a waterfall, but I don't care.

"Rachel," Mrs. Price says. She says it like she's getting mad. "You put that sweater on right now and no more nonsense."

"But it's not—"

"Now!" Mrs. Price says.

This is when I wish I wasn't eleven, because all the years inside of me—ten, nine, eight, seven, six, five, four, three, two, and one—are pushing at the back of my eyes when I put one arm through one sleeve of the sweater that smells like cottage cheese, and then the other arm through the other and stand there with my arms apart like if the sweater hurts me and it does, all itchy and full of germs that aren't even mine.

That's when everything I've been holding in since this morning, since when Mrs. Price put the sweater on my desk, finally lets go, and all of a sudden I'm crying in front of everybody. I wish I was invisible but I'm not. I'm eleven and it's my birthday today and I'm crying like I'm three in front of everybody. I put my head down on the desk and bury my face in my stupid clown-sweater arms. My face all hot and spit coming out of my mouth because I can't stop the little animal noises from coming out of me, until there aren't any more tears left in my eyes, and it's just my body shaking like when you have the hiccups, and my whole head hurts like when you drink milk too fast.

But the worst part is right before the bell rings for lunch. That stupid Phyllis Lopez, who is even dumber than Sylvia Saldivar, says she remembers the red sweater is hers! I take it off right away and give it to her, only Mrs. Price pretends like everything's okay.

Today I'm eleven. There's a cake Mama's making for tonight, and when Papa comes home from work we'll eat it. There'll be candles and presents and everyone will sing Happy birthday, happy birthday to you, Rachel, only it's too late.

I'm eleven today. I'm eleven, ten, nine, eight, seven, six, five, four, three, two, and one, but I wish I was one hundred and two. I wish I was anything but eleven, because I want today to be far away already, far away like a runaway balloon, Like a tiny o *in the sky, so tiny-tiny you have to close your eyes to see it.*

No matter how old we are or how different, each of us has her beginning years to share, think, talk, and write about. Like you, Rachel has a right to be listened to and to feel safe expressing what's on her mind, especially when it's personal. I'm glad Sandra Cisneros wrote about Rachel's painful experience because it helps us realize we're not alone. Each of us experiences pain growing up, especially when isms affect how people treat children.

What's Different, What's the Same

I am going to be forty-seven years old, and I am being reborn. —*Rebecca*

Have you noticed that adults don't tell their age, yet they expect children and teenagers to tell how old they are? The girls and women in the workshop are like Rebecca; we introduce ourselves by revealing our ages and something we want the group to know about us, something the other girls and women in the room probably couldn't guess by looking at us. As women tell their ages, it surprises some girls. One time, one of the girls said "Whoa" after each woman revealed her age, and she made us laugh after a few "Whoas." Sometimes what we think an age looks like isn't what someone that age really looks like. Maybe girls and women don't always tell their ages because people behave as if girls aren't valuable when they're very young and women are worth less as they get old. That's what ageism does. It makes it taboo to tell your age, as if being young or old is embarrassing. I've learned from girls that knowing a woman who has

Insights

It's challenging to figure out what you want someone to know about you that they couldn't guess. What is important to you that you want other people to know but isn't easy to see? Making a list of words that describe you and a list of words that describe what you like to do could reveal what is unique about you. Compare the two lists and determine how much of your true self is easy to see. How do you feel about your conclusion? Remember, you decide what you want people to know about you.

lived as her true self all her life shows them they can look forward to getting older. Meeting women who enjoy being different reminds us that there is more than one way to be happy.

Janine, who's thirteen, asked why her age surprised everyone. It was because she's so tall, and most people assumed her height means she's grown-up. She thought she had to act older, and it was funny to think she was expected to "act her height" as well as her age.

When I say I'm sixty, girls are usually very surprised because that seems so old to them. *I'm* surprised that I've been alive for so many years, too. I used to think life stopped when you got old, and now I'm learning it keeps getting new as long as I listen to my inner voice. When I say that being nine or ten means knowing what's fair and thinking you can be anything you want to be, most girls agree, especially girls who are at or close to those ages. Introducing yourself this way—telling both your age and something you want others to know about you—challenges ageism and stereotypes about appearances. I hope you will feel comfortable using this type of introduction whenever you can.

Differences

Here are some examples of what some girls say make them unique. One eleven-year-old girl living in the USA is adopted from China, and her connection to two different cultures is something special about her. Another girl's parents are divorced, and she wants to use her mother's and her father's last names to show she comes from both of them. Another girl has a disabled sister, and she's learned from her sister that disabled people are like anyone else.

Girls in various parts of the world do a lot of things that may not fit popular ideas about being female but are true to who they are: one girl rides horses; another studies karate; some girls read a lot; and some girls play sports, including basketball, boxing, soccer, softball, volleyball, surfing, mountain climbing, and football. Two sisters who grew up in a coastal town on the small island of Trinidad, where they were born, recently moved to New York City. You can imagine what an amazing list they can share of what's different about their daily lives now. A sixteen-year-old girl lives in an apartment in a public housing development in Chicago, and she doesn't feel safe going outside alone except to go to school. One girl in the Ukraine has a boyfriend and another girl wants one. Some girls aren't really interested in boys yet. One fifteen-year-old girl likes being with girls better than boys and says she has felt that way for as long as she can remember.

A woman in South Carolina wants to be better connected with her thirteen-year-old daughter. Another woman in South Carolina, a teacher and a minister named Helen, was the first black student to go to a state college. She grew up in an all-black town because white people had segregated the state—that is, they wouldn't let black people live where white people lived—but she had benefited from being with other black people who had accepted her as a black girl. Being with white people when she went away to college was new to her. She was shocked to realize that they didn't like her: she was actually hit by water from high-pressure hoses as she walked into a school building by whites who didn't want her in the same college with them. The first night she was away at school, the police told her she had to sleep in the jail in order to be safe. She still remembers that the police didn't let her call her family, and her parents worried all night because they didn't know where she was. That still makes her angry today, but she would do it again because "everyone deserves the best education."

Natalie, a ten-year-old girl, read a story about an African-American boy who was a slave during the Civil War. Natalie couldn't understand why people are cruel to other people just because of their color. "It doesn't make sense to me. It's not logical that people care so much about skin color," she said. Skin color is something girls talk about when we look at a group of girls and women like those in your picture collection or in a workshop.

Similarities

When I was in a Chicago workshop, everyone in the room except me was African-American, and when I asked the girls to talk about what was the same about us, Kayla, who is twelve years old, surprised me by saying, "We're all black." For a moment, it was quiet in the room. Then one of the women said, "No, Andrea's white." Kayla just shrugged her shoulders and said, "Oh, I thought she was light-skinned." It's good to be with people from different races—you understand more about how we all experience things. Your world gets bigger, and you learn that there's less to be afraid of and more to enjoy about each other than people imagine before you step outside your neighborhood or town.

Check In Looking Inside and Out

When I ask what's different about the people in a group of females, girls usually list all the different styles and colors of clothes and different types of shoes. When you think about what's different about you and girls you know best, like sisters or friends, what kinds of things come to mind? Is it mostly things we can see like body size, hairstyles, and clothes? Do you imagine we're different on the inside? What differences and similarities would you list?

Females are the most common victims of sexism, so most of us will experience it at some time. We can overcome sexism, though, like Helen did when she integrated a college. (The opposite of "segregate," which is about keeping people apart, is "integrate," which means to bring people together, like blacks going to college with whites.) Each victory against prejudice begins with one person's actions. When many people believe in the same thing, they start a movement. I belong to the Feminist Movement because I believe in equality for girls, women, boys, and men.

You can keep these thoughts in mind as you read what other females believe. Their words may help you express yourself.

Finding Memorable Females

As a girl, I didn't learn what's powerful about women from textbooks or classroom discussions because female human beings were rarely mentioned in what I studied. The idea that there are girls who do memorable things wasn't even considered! But I did have some great women teachers who cared about me and understood me more than anyone else did. My seventh-grade and eighth-grade teacher (I had the same teacher for two years) and my high school teacher were both female, and they showed me that there could be something special and exciting about being a woman, including reaching out to girls. One of those teachers, my middle school teacher, Arlene, even helped with this book by suggesting stories for girls to read.

Are there any girls or women who inspire you? Girls often say they want to talk to and trust women. One young woman said her father had raised her not to trust women because her mother had left him when she was three. She was glad to meet women in this book who made her feel good about herself and becoming a woman. We find women different ways: sometimes they're our mothers or in our family, sometimes they're teachers, sometimes they're women we meet in workshops, and sometimes they're women we see in movies, in television programs, on websites, and/or in books and magazines who help us believe we're okay and not alone.

How many women or girls can you remember learning about from history books or classroom discussions? When I ask this question in workshops, we usually discover that there are very few females written about in history, especially females of color and girls. Even the pictures on walls in auditoriums, school hallways, and classrooms are generally of white men like the ones called the Founding Fathers. In fact, girls and women are over half the human population, and our gender is part of everything that happens. As one girl said, "I want girls to finally be treated as equals. We need to learn how to get the power around to girls and women."

Females are missing from history books and discussions, but it's not because we didn't do anything important. We're missing from history because people who write the textbooks—and many teachers and people who make decisions about what's important in history—leave us out. That's why there's no mention of the fact that there were places and times when females shared or took control in matriarchal (woman-led) Native American tribes, for example, and no mention of females' contributions to their communities. That's one of the reasons why I put girls' and women's writings from each Girls Speak Out workshop into a small book, which you'll read more about later. Everyone who attends at least one workshop gets a copy. It's a new way to record history, and it grew into this book.

Nine-year-old Karen in New York said, "All those history books in school and libraries are written without us." Twelve-year-old Anna in Fiji agreed: "Boys already have history written down for them, and it's in their favor because we live in male-dominated countries." But when we write down our unique experiences, we see that they are now history, too. Your notebook is one of the first notebooks in which girls challenge isms and begin to trust their power.

Isn't it amazing that having different kinds of experiences is something we girls and women have in common with each other? At the same time, our personal opinions and insights, our special stories, help make each of us a special and unique female. Instead of being afraid of our differences—which can happen when girls believe stereotypes that say black girls are tough and like to fight or white girls are clueless and weak, or when girls are ashamed of physical or emotional similarities such as having a period or weeping openly—we have a right to respect our unique selves. When we do this, we are helping to get "the power around to girls and women." We *are* history and we are *making* history.

CLAIMING OUR HISTORY

I feel like me when I take a stand. —Kathryn

Remember, history is happening right this very second, but it disappears with each second unless we decide to remember and record what happened. Then we can give it a name, just like we name ourselves. Historians use words like "revolution" or "movement" when a lot of people decide to solve a problem they're tired of living with. In addition, we can write history to record the feelings of a Mexican-American girl turning eleven at the end of the twentieth century. That's what Sandra Cisneros did. Her kind of history includes individual history (the history of one individual), which is what we are making with each of our lives. Even if it's not written down, the history of each girl's and woman's life is important.

Our story as a human race began thousands of years ago, a long time before books or notebooks existed. How does a girl learn without books? The same way Kayla in Chicago does when she looks around a room; she looks, thinks, and says what's on her mind. She's making her own observations. She's a historian. We can look back at remnants of ancient times, too. Cave paintings were an early way of recording what seemed important and memorable in everyday life a very long time ago. Ruins of ancient buildings and statues teach us history, too. Telling the stories of a tribe or a group of people out loud is called oral history; that is, it passes from generation to generation from spoken memory.

Prehistory

Prehistory is the name given to the experiences of people who lived before what we call writing was invented. Prehistory existed before *patriarchy*. A patriarchy is a system in which men dominate women and children. All of us on earth—children, women, men, and nature—are living in a patriarchy now. It has been the system for the last five thousand years or so, depending on which part of the world you live in—but that's much less than the 5 percent of the time that people have been on earth.

Today, we're only taught written history so it's easy to forget about prehistory and mistakenly think a patriarchy is the "natural" and "normal" way for human beings to live. Because a patriarchy is created to favor males, many of its customs or rules are unfair to females. But 95 percent of human history happened in prehistory, before there were books, and we're learning more and more from ruins, bones, cave paintings, and oral legends—many unwritten things. These things reveal a time before patriarchy when females had as much power as males, and sometimes even more. True!

Supposed-Tos

Girls discuss a lot of supposed-tos in this book that are part of the current patriarchal system. A supposed-to can be a rule that's written down. It can be an unwritten rule that people tell each other. A supposed-to is something we're told we should want to do, especially in a patriarchal society, but it doesn't always feel right. For instance, some girls feel they should pretend they're not as smart as boys in school so boys will like them or not make fun of them. When girls act against a stereotype, when they don't follow a supposed-to, they may be teased. This is because the people who tease don't want girls to express their true selves. There's nothing wrong with girls who go right ahead and challenge the patriarchal system, acting as if a fair system, not one that favors boys and men, is in control. In fact, girls who act as if females are equal to males are role models for females and males of any age who want to live in a fair system.

It's easy to become confused, as I was as a child, and think there is something wrong with you because so many people still go along with the unfair system. I liked knowing the answers in school, especially when I had tried hard to figure things out, but I remember sitting there knowing boys would be called on before— and more often than— any of the girls. And that it was more okay for them to argue or say what they thought.

Most written history is about people living in patriarchal societies and it confuses many girls and women and makes us feel invisible. But prehistory is filled with other possibilities. There are surprises in imagining possibilities. Have you ever heard of Wonder Woman? She has super powers and uses them to help people. She is a comic book heroine from the USA, dressed in red, white, and blue, but she's also an example of how we can go into the past of any country and create ideas for a new present and future. As you'll see, even a modern comic book figure had a beginning in prehistory.

Wonder Woman has a mission, to change "a world torn by the hatreds and wars of men." She does it without killing her

Your Landmarks

Paint or sketch a map of your village, town, or neighborhood. Locate your favorite place at the center, and name it after yourself. Imagine it's fifty years in the future and you are a visitor looking for signs that show the strengths of girls and women. Using numbers and a key that explains what each number is, name all the artifacts or remains that indicate the power of females. For example, a library called The Wonders of Girls and Women could be next door to an all-girls' School of Science and Technology that just happens to be named after your best friend. There may be places for boys and men; however, you decide whether to limit it to female landmarks. We can look behind us to the Amazons, for instance, for stories about wonderful females or ahead in our imaginations for stories about ourselves or people we know.

enemies. Wonder Woman believes in peace, equality, self-reliance, and respect for others. What's "historical" about her is that she's modeled on an Amazon, a member of what may have been a race of superhuman women from thousands of years ago who lived in different parts of the world.

As my friend Gloria wrote in an introduction to a book about the origins of Wonder Woman, "There's . . . evidence . . . Amazon societies were real; they did exist. . . . In the jungles of Brazil, German and Brazilian scientists found caves of what appears to have been an all-female society. . . . Such myths and archaeological finds have turned up not only along the Amazon River in Brazil, but at the foot of the Atlas Mountains in northwestern

Africa, and on the European and Asiatic sides of the Black Sea. . . .

"Rather than give up freedom [when patriarchy began to rule women] and worship only male gods, some bands of women resisted. They formed all-women cultures . . . In Europe, graves once thought to contain male skeletons—because they were buried with weapons, or killed by battle wounds—have turned out to contain skeletons of females after all."

The ideas that women are weak and can't govern themselves are myths and part of patriarchy, not accurate historical facts. Wonder Woman is based on life before patriarchy. Like Gloria, when we write or talk about the lives of females, we can include facts that show they have been strong since prehistory. Females have been powerful throughout history, too.

Lucy

One of the earliest human skeletons found by scientists is of an African woman; those who found her named her Lucy. She's thousands of years old, but she did a lot of the same wonderful things we do today: she walked on the same earth under the same sky, she had a family, and she wondered about her future. Our skin colors evolved from Lucy's color, which was black, to all the different shades we see around us today.

If we travel back to Lucy's lifetime, we find that she spent most of her time with many other girls and women because males went off and hunted together. (Remember, without us, there would be no history or human race!) Just as we do, Lucy saw females around her get older, go from place to place, and change in size and shape. She watched sunsets and sunrises, she could see the moon appear to swallow the sun during a total eclipse, and she saw crescent moons, half moons, and full moons.

At night, sleeping outside, moonlight would shine on Lucy's face like a night-light. As the moon changed shape, from a sliver to a full moon, it would shine different amounts of light on her face. It takes about a month for the moon to go through its cycles, from crescent to full. A girl like Lucy, living thousands of years ago, would have noticed something that happened to the girls and women around her on earth that corresponded to the phases of the moon in the heavens.

Once a month, some girls and women would bleed—but they weren't hurt, and they didn't die. Month after month, they had these menstrual periods (named periods because they're periodic, or cyclic), and they would bleed and be okay. Menstruation was magic. It happened with a rhythmic cycle similar to the cycle of the moon. I think Lucy must have believed that there's a connection between our ability to menstruate and something far away in the sky. It isn't a connection we can see or touch, but it's something that we can imagine has special meaning, and it gives us a special connection to something big and important, like the way the earth turns in its solar system.

Perhaps Lucy welcomed having her period because it made her feel powerful enough to connect with the moon in the sky. Today girls have different experiences with their periods. A girl in San Diego, California, asked Girls Speak Out participants at one workshop if it makes any difference how old a girl is before she starts her period. Each female in the room had started menstruating at a different age, from nine to fifteen years old. One girl wants to design a cramps doll to hold in your hand and squeeze when you have cramps. Girls say they have to hide tampons and sanitary napkins in their backpacks and pockets because it would be embarrassing if boys found them. They feel ashamed of having their period, and they keep their time of the month a secret. When one group is supposed to be superior—such as men, who don't bleed each month—then whatever happens to the other group—females, who bleed monthly—is considered inferior.

Wow, Things Can Change!

That's the way things are now for most females, but some of us have been doing things to change what's unfair. What would it be like if sexist beliefs changed? Let's imagine that women didn't get their periods, but men did. Gloria wrote an article in which she wondered what would happen "If Men Could Menstruate?" If men are considered superior, would getting a period just be something else that's considered superior, too? If they got their periods, Gloria decided, "Men would brag about how long and how much.

"Young boys would talk about it as the envied beginning of manhood. Gifts, religious ceremonies, family dinners and . . . parties would mark the day. . . ." Doing reversals, like Alice in Wonderland's walking in the wrong direction to get to the right place, is one of the ways we can change how we understand things. All you have to do is imagine that something being said to you was being said to a boy, or something said about white people was said about people of color.

Can you imagine celebrating your period? We don't have to imagine ourselves back in Lucy's time to find people who celebrate menstruation. Native American girls and women come from very old cultures, and they have ceremonies to mark a girl's period and welcome this new part of her life. Gina, a mother of two girls in northern California, worked with a group of girls and me in designing Girls Speak Out. She thought the idea of celebrating your period was a good one, so when her older daughter, Cathy, got her period, Gina and her husband and younger daughter gave

Cathy gifts and took her out to dinner. Carla, the younger daughter, is looking forward to her celebration.

Cathy's friend Denise heard about celebrating your period and said, "It sure beats getting a bottle of aspirin thrown at you." That's what happened to Denise when she told her parents she had her first period.

Unfortunately, menstruation is often treated as if it's a problem, something to be embarrassed about or ashamed of—as if it's taboo or a secret—for no reason except that it only happens to females. (A taboo is something that we're told not to talk about because it's bad.) Sometimes a girl learns about menstruation from another girl. That's how I learned: my cousin, who is six months older than I am, told me all about it when she got her period, and when I told my mother, she gave me a booklet to read that was written by a company that makes sanitary napkins. Most girls are shocked when I explain that our periods gradually stop for women, usually in their late forties and early fifties—during what's called *menopause*. Our periods don't last our whole lives; they only happen during the years we can have a baby, if we want to.

Now you have a chance to read a conversation between two friends about getting their period. You can read out loud or silently. This time it's from a novel called *Brown Girl, Brownstones* by Paule Marshall. In this excerpt, twelve-year-old Selina has strong reactions when her best friend, Beryl, tells her she has her period and that another of their friends, Ina, has hers, too. Selina hasn't gotten her period yet, and she doesn't know what it is even though she's as old as some girls who are menstruating. Many girls experience the same confusion as Selina. I did, too, because my mother didn't want to talk about very personal things at all.

Beryl and Selina are talking in the park one afternoon, near their homes in Brooklyn, New York. When Beryl tells Selina, "I bleed sometimes," Selina's first reaction is to say, "So what. Everybody does." Beryl explains that she bleeds . . .

"Not from a cut or anything but from below. Where the baby pops out. Ina does, too. That's why she gets pains every once in a while. I'll tell you, if you want to hear . . ."

"Tell me." And beneath [Selina's] eagerness there was dread.

Beryl raised up, gathering her dress neatly under her. Her eyes flitted nervously across Selina's intense face. Then, with her head bowed and a squeamish look she explained it all. "That's why I'm getting these things," she concluded, jabbing her small breasts. "It happens to all girls."

Selina stared very quietly at her and, for that moment, she was quiet inside, her whole self suspended in disbelief. Then an inexplicable revulsion gripped her and her face screwed with disgust. "It's never going to happen to me," she said proudly.

"It'll happen. It hurts sometimes and it makes you miserable in the summer . . ."

"Well, if it ever happens to me nobody'll ever know. They'll see me change and think it's magic."

"Besides, it makes you feel important."

"How could anyone walking around dripping blood feel important?"

"It's funny but you do. Almost as if you were grown up. It's like . . . oh, it's hard to explain to a kid . . ."

"Who's a kid?"

"You, because you haven't started yet."

"I'll never start!" And beneath her violent denial there was despair.

"Oh yes, you'll start." Beryl nodded wisely. "Wait, lemme try to explain how it makes you feel. The first time I was scared. Then I began to feel different. That's it. Even though nothing's changed

and I still play kid games and go around with kids, even though my best friend's a kid"—she bowed to Selina—"I feel different. Like I'm carrying something secret and special inside. . . ."

Selina says she's "still trapped within a hard flat body." She closed her eyes to hide the tears and was safe momentarily from Beryl and Ina and all the others joined against her in their cult of blood and breasts.

After a time Beryl came and lay close to her. She placed her arm comfortingly around her. "What was that poem you wrote about the sky?" she asked. And always her voice calmed Selina. Her disappointment, her anguish tapered slowly until finally her tears were gone and she turned to Beryl and held her. . . . "It wasn't about this kind of sky," she said and began to recite, her thin voice striking the rock and veering off into the sky, her eyes closed, her face serene in sleep. Whispering, Selina recited then to the rock, to the dome of sky, to the light wind, all the poems she had scribbled in class, that came bright and vivid at night.

Beryl stirred in her sleep and pressed Selina closer. Just then the sun rose above the rock. The strong light seemed to smooth the grass, to set the earth steaming richly. They were all joined it seemed: Beryl with the blood bursting each month inside her; the sun, the seared grass and earth—even she, though barren of breasts, was part of the mosaic.

When Selina is looking up at the sky, I think she has a lot of different feelings all at once. Maybe Lucy felt the same way. Without written words from Lucy's era to tell us how she felt about getting her period, we can only imagine what she felt. That's another reason it's important for you to think of history as females having similar experiences. Did Lucy feel left out, the way Selina did at first, or did she welcome it? Your answer about Lucy's feelings is as important as the answer a scientist imagines.

A Period Is a Beginning

How do you feel about having a period? What feelings do/did you have as you wait(ed) for your first period? How did you learn about females and their periods? Design an invitation to a party celebrating your period. You might write your feelings about getting your period in your notebook. Maybe you have a friend who also wants to talk or write about menstruation or menopause.

A friend of mine who is Chinese-American didn't know that it's natural to begin bleeding at a certain time of the month, and when she found blood on her panties, she thought she was dying. She wrote a will and left her toys and books to her sisters. When she had a daughter, she was sure to explain what happens to a girl's body when it begins to change physically. How would you explain menstruation to a younger girl? What could you say that would make her feel like she belongs to a powerful tradition?

We can imagine almost anything, for instance, the very different way we might feel if we believed the truth that there is something exciting and powerful about being a female. You might feel differently about female genitals, too, if we didn't live in a culture that often makes them seem dirty or shameful. Just think about the slang words for this magical part of the body. Gloria and I have been trying to think of a new name for female genitals because so many of the names sound bad or weak, especially when they're used as curses or insults. We thought about *power bundle*.

Maybe you, too, have some suggestions to add to your notebook or share with a friend.

When girls and women are remembered as equal to boys and men, we will be moving closer to a system that is fair to each girl, woman, boy, and man.

New Voices

I am a symbol of other women.

—Jabethea

The idea that it's special to be female is not new. In researching prehistory, I traveled back in time to almost two hundred thousand years ago.

I discovered that many more images of females have been found than of males. Artifacts or objects from prehistory are mostly of women because of a woman's magical power of gestation, birth, and generating food from her body. For instance, a child's grave was found from two hundred thousand years ago covered by a slab of stone. Carved on the underside of the stone, facing up toward the child's body, are pairs of breasts. These carvings were a way of protecting the child. Breast-shaped carvings as images of power are found throughout prehistory.

Female Artifacts

The first human artifacts I've found copies of that we can actually hold in our hands are from thirty-seven thousand years ago. They are images of female human beings, and they're believed to be guardians of the earth. They have no feet, and they were stuck upright in the ground. You can see what they looked like in the section titled "About the Ancient Artifacts" toward the back of this book. These small statues were used to remind people of the female's mysterious power to create and care for life on earth.

I wasn't surprised, just disappointed, when I read in a popular book on prehistory that despite the fact that most early artifacts are of women, the book only included a picture of a male artifact. It made me want to have something special from prehistory to show girls and women. Wouldn't it be great if we could at least see, feel, and touch exact copies of a lot of early female artifacts?

I decided to collect copies of artifacts of girls and women from prehistory. I wanted the collection to include figures from all seven continents. Then we could see them in this book, and in workshops we could hold and touch them; we could decide for ourselves what other possibilities there are for female human beings as if they were always free to develop their power.

The artifacts I collected can't talk, of course, but they are a valuable part of Girls Speak Out. You can imagine what they would say if they could talk. They're no longer lost voices because you share your voice with them.

It's a special moment when we see many artifacts of females together for the first time, as they are at the end of this book. It may be similar to what you felt when you completed your picture collection. Look at the drawings of the artifacts in this book; how do you feel about the different ways female bodies can look? Some are thin, some are fat, some have big breasts or big behinds, and some are small all over—just like the variety of girls in your imagination and in your picture collection. Some of the Girls Speak Out artifacts are made of clay, some are wood, and some are painted with bright colors while others are carved from gray stone. Look at the description beneath each drawing to find out where each artifact was found and a theory about how she was used.

Cindy is a grandmother who came to a workshop in North Carolina. She believes it's "important to see that artifacts came in different sizes and shapes and that there was a beauty to each of them." Cindy is now "more conscious of being accepting of how I look, and I think we need to be loyal to one another regardless of what we look like."

Introducing the Artifacts

As you read about the artifacts, remember that you can join in by creating your own artifact story. It's exciting to give the artifacts a voice. You might use pictures instead of words to express what you think an artifact would say. You can be creative in a variety of ways.

For instance, a nine-year-old girl, Ruth, confided to an older girl that she couldn't read or write, so the older girl wrote down her story. If you want to share parts of this book with a very young girl, perhaps you can record what she says and then read it for her. Ruth surprised us when she decided to read her story out loud, word by word, by repeating after another reader. Ruth had trouble reading and writing because she wasn't taught at home and she didn't go to school often—the adults in her house didn't care about school, so it was hard for her to get up and be ready with clean clothes in time for the school bus. A group of girls around her age looked out for her and made sure she got to the Girls

Uncovering Voices

You can welcome an ancient artifact by giving her a voice. Search for an artifact you like from the pictures on these pages, and imagine her story or *herstory*, which some people use as another word for "history." You can write an essay, a poem, a newspaper article, or an email message. You decide. Try to imagine what memories of herstory she's holding inside her that you can set free. Is she feeling angry and is she waiting to express her anger? Has she had a happy or sad experience in her village?

Girls have all kinds of ideas about the artifacts' history. Sometimes looking at the expression on a face or the way she holds her body or dresses are clues we can use in a story. If an artifact has an unusual appearance such as one with no face, her story can explain that fact.

Remember, the artifacts are from a time when there was no written language so there are no records of what they represented or what their stories were. Nine-year-old Leah from Canada thinks, "There's a lot more imagining for us to do here because it's not written down." Girls' and women's stories about the artifacts are collected below. When you read what girls and women have written, they may inspire you. You can read their stories about the artifacts before you write, as you write, or after you're finished writing.

Speak Out workshops. Being there helped Ruth to know that not going to school regularly wasn't her fault, and it didn't mean she couldn't use her intelligence.

Not all girls have time to read this book or have the ability to travel to a workshop, even with the help of friends. In some parts of the world, in large and small countries, girls work to support their families instead of going to school or workshops. Some cultures forbid females from learning, especially about reading and writing, because they may discover their power. Sharing powerful words about females is an important thing to do, and I wish all girls could share their wisdom and the wisdom they find in these artifacts.

Another girl who was eleven told me her artifact story was going to be hard for me to understand because she has a learning problem. She's dyslexic, which means it's hard for her to see or write letters in order, and she's uncomfortable asking for help. After explaining her difficulties with writing, she dictated her story to me.

Some girls had the opposite problem—they were very good in school, but they had only learned how to repeat what other people had done, not how to use their imagination. They had an easy time reading and writing, but they took longer to reach inside themselves. No matter what, girls wanted to speak out and give these ancient artifacts a new voice.

Girls who enjoy being in front of a group often have someone hold their artifact while they talk to her as well as about her. If you'd like to hear your story read aloud, perhaps you and a friend can be the spoken voices for a pair of artifacts. Some girls don't want their story read out loud, but they do want their story printed in the small book I put together about their workshop. Most girls do want their stories in their workshop book as long as I change their name to protect their privacy.

Take time to imagine where your chosen artifact lived, what her family was like, and how she felt about being female. Many girls write about the way males treated an artifact. You can spend as much time as you need creating facts and details for your story.

The following section features actual words written by girls and women who have attended Girls Speak Out workshops or read this book. I think you'll like the names the girls have given to the artifacts. Some girls and women called the little statues by their own names, some made up names, and others felt they didn't need names, but each person told what a female artifact might say if she had the power to say what she really felt. Reading these stories may inspire you.

A Young Girl with Four Arms

Once upon a time
I was a little young girl
with four arms and
I was holding the sun
to help my people see better
and be black like me.
And I will make clothes
for my people and
jewelry and bracelets.
They will be gold bracelets
and some silver
but I will feed my people
and I will give them a wish.
And I will make some coats
for raining and boats for snowing
and give them combs and brushes
to do their ponytails
and give them
crowns to make them
kings and queens.

Tabethea

by Tabethea, 15

My name is Tabethea. I am special. I don't have to wear clothes because no one else wears clothes. I am a symbol of other women. I walk and talk just as you do, but I do not wear the clothes that you do, but I go undressed because I'm comfortable just as you are in your clothes. I live from day to day the same as you do.

The only thing that's different is the animals I eat to get nourishment. The symbol I hold in my hand is to call on whichever animal I choose to eat. I am overweight, but it does not bother me because you do not have to live in my body. I'm very comfortable with the way I look. I had many children, which is most of the reason I am this way. But you women in this day and age are very tuned into the way you dress and the way you look, but there's no difference between you and I because we are both women.

BACK OFF

by Toni, 13

Back off. Leave me alone. I can't believe what you punks did to me. You thought I was nothing, but you were wrong. Yes, I'm back, you bully, and mad as heck. I cried and screamed giving birth to your children. You just threw me in a hole with no history, excuse me, her-story. I hope you fear me.

I fed you, clothed you, and took care of you. This is the thanks I get. You are a creature me and my sisters made. You are a man. I loved and respected you, but you dissed me. I am coming to your house and I'm going to stretch myself, play cards with the fellas, and have you wait on me hand and foot. But it's not going to happen because you made me without a mouth. That's because you fear me. Then I must have power. My sisters will find you men and diss you, my brother.

Destiny

Her name is Destiny. She's totally naked, but not embarrassed about it. Her hands are sitting on her large beautiful breasts to draw attention to her body. Also, Destiny has no face because she doesn't need one. Even without a face, even without a mouth, you can still hear her roar. Destiny is proud and powerful. She represents all women because we are all different, but all the same.

by Brazley, 13

My Artifact

by Jeneil, 9

My artifact, I believe, is an African queen. She believes that all people are no different. They may be richer, poorer, but she keeps her faith and her beliefs. She keeps strong and when she wants something done, she tries, does not give up. She tries not to fail. A woman is no greater than a man, but we have the power to give life. Women have the dream about things they could never talk about with a man.

Every woman has a gift to give. Women, black or white, could talk together and talk about children and different things. No woman should be afraid of a man because we have a great power men do not have. That's what I feel about being a woman.

by Lizard, 11

I am a young girl of long ago. I live in a time when no one had heard of sexism. Men and women are equal in everything they do. I can express my feelings in any way I want to. If I am really excited they do not tell me to calm down. I'm trapped inside a young girl of today. I cannot let out my feelings. No one even knows I exist. I feel like I am dead. For only dead people should not be free.

That is their bodies that are limp while their spirits dance and play in the air. Please set me free to be who I am and what I want to be. Don't keep me trapped. I'm only here for the public's eye, not for myself. Let me dance and play in the wind and rain. Let me love my friends and cherish nature. If I should kiss a snail, don't have people laugh at me and say how disgusting I am.

I am myself, not another person's property, so I'll let my feelings out so much, and really cry and laugh and do anything that I want to do. I miss the world, the happiness, and the joy that I once had. Get me free through your laughter and your tears, and don't be afraid to show your love to another person. No matter what other people think of them. Let me live free!

by Monzerrat, 10

Los de madera son de Africa. Y los de madera siempre se peliában el uno con el otro. Y una dia uno se escapó y los ostros estaban riéndose, pero el se cayó empieza llorar y los ostros que estaban riéndose se cayeron también. Y el que se cayó primero estaba riéndose y como vivien juntos se separaron cada uno y comian juntos pero no dormian juntos. Y juguban y mataban animals para comer, como bufalos, peces o venado y comian maiz y ostras cosas diferentes. Y el cuero de los bufalos o venado lo usaban para ropa y cosas diferentes como zapatos y dibujos. Lo estiriban para pintar y con la fruta hacian pintura, con naranja y frutos. Y cuando otras personas illegáron les enseñáron a plantar y a los niños les enseñáron juegos y cosas neuvas y a plantar cosas neuvas.

The wooden ones from Africa

by Monzerrat, 10

The wooden ones are from Africa. And they often fought one another. And one day one escaped from the others. They were laughing, but the one that fell down began to cry and the ones that were laughing fell down, too. And the one that fell first was laughing, and since they lived together, they separated and ate together. But they didn't sleep together. And they played and killed animals to eat like buffaloes, fish, and deer. And they ate corn and other things and used the hide for clothing and things like shoes and drawings. They stretched it to paint on and with oranges and fruit they made paint. And when other people came, they showed them how to plant and they showed the children games and new things and how to plant things.

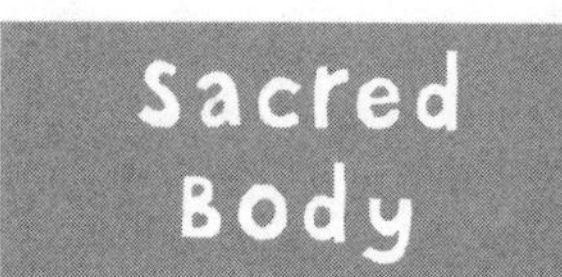

She wraps her arms tightly around her body because her body is sacred to her. She is able to do things that no man can—the most important, being able to bring new life into this world. She looks into the sky and thinks to herself that the world can be a better place for her and her children if we work together.

by Jiffany, 26

The Old Day

This woman's name is Kauo. Kauo is an old woman. She's about twenty thousand years old. She's a strong woman because she has a snake on her head and she's holding a globe. She uses her power by rubbing her globe. When she holds her globe, she limps over.

During the day, she feeds her snake. She wears a long dress, a big necklace and she wears her hair in a ponytail. Kauo lives by herself. She lives in Africa. Kauo is a mean lady. She's the meanest lady in Africa.

by Shamika, 9

Two-Spirited Goddess

by Mary, 43

This is the two-spirited goddess of fertility. Her name is Frog Woman. Two-Spirited. She is woman and man. She claims a woman's power to bring forth life. The village prays to Frog Woman for rain. Rain means life for the village. It means food to make the body strong to bring forth life.

Frog Woman tells women to take control of our bodies. She tells us to be self-assured and confident in our power. She tells us to love our bodies and the source of our power.

Grandmother

by Serinna, 12

Once upon a time there was a group of women. They would catch fish all day so they could eat. The biggest woman got to be the queen because she was the warmest and the safest.

But one day she fell asleep, and they couldn't wake her up. Then they got a bell and she woke up. The ladies told her they were going for a swim. Grandmother was asleep again and it was even harder to wake her up. They rang the bell for a longer time than they did before, and it finally woke her up.

Each time grandmother fell asleep it was harder to wake her up. When she fell asleep, everybody would all lay around her and restore her warmth. And they would sing her awake.

Tamer of Horses

by Joanna, 9

While each part of my body was being carved into the wall, I felt happy because I felt like I was coming to life, but when I was taken out it felt like I was being killed.

The horses are my companions. They are the only ones who understand me. I am the only one who understands them.

First I was carved because I was the first ever to communicate with horses. The horses are my friends, but they were also the first horses ever to like a human. From then on horses were known as carefree and happy.

I've got a message for all you people out there: girls are as good as boys and girls can do the same things.

I know because everyone teased me about trying to tame horses, but now everyone is thanking me for absolutely everything.

My life ended peacefully, burned and buried.

Saferia

by Abigail, 15

"Saferia": (sah-fear-ah) one of strength, essence, and beauty.

Saferia was one of the beauties in a relatively small town in India. Everything about her represents a lot of what she is, but can be easily misread, like most women today.

Saferia was created with darkly outlined eyes to emphasize or more likely to symbolize the windows to her soul. The more you look into them and try to understand them and what they try to say, the more bewildered and interested you are in knowing how to decipher the language and answer in the same way.

Her long hair represents her beauty, and yet adds to her strength and mystery. It gives her a sexuality all her own. Her feline ways are expressed through the cat on her head. She is agile, witty, curious, intelligent, quick, and always lands on her feet.

Her face displays her willingness to love only those who are deserving.

Her figure and breasts serve as a temporary holding place for a carefree, loving, and insatiable spirit. Her spirit is trapped inside looking for its counterpart to set her free.

Her beauty is where her strength is because it's natural. It's not doctored or created, but enhanced by her soul. What is natural is undeniable and unstoppable. When something cannot be stopped, it is strong.

Her beauty also serves as a defense. It protects her from the ugliness around her, the nature of man.

Tall, fair, and beautiful, with a smile like the sun.
Her hips like songs waiting to be sung.
Her eyes like wounds, full of much pain.
Her lips wet and perfectly round like pellets of rain.
Her hair like roots searching for earth.
Her breasts stand out, ready to give birth,
Give birth to her heart and soul.
Her body holds her spirit one and whole.
She is like a story waiting to be told.
Her heart is up for sale, waiting to be sold . . .

Mujer Palo

Ella es de Africa. Ella es grande. No tiene manos pero si tiene pies y tiene noventa años y es flaquita. Es bonita. Tiene su cara pintada. Tiene cuello grande es una mujer fuerte. La pintura representa algo, un simbolo de mujere grande y fuerte.

by Bertha, 12

by Kila, 10

Once upon a time I was a spiritual woman. I was also faithful to my people. I was hurt when people made fun of my spiritual life. My clothes were made of the finest silk in town. I lived all alone in a small house in the village.

In my country, angels walk with women and watch over men.

I was born with the ability to carve in wood. Then I became famous for my beautiful sculptures.

And Angel is my famous name.

Woman of Wood

by Bertha, 10

She's from Africa. She is big. She doesn't have hands, but she does have feet and she's ninety years old and is thin. She's pretty. She has a painted face. She has a big neck and is a strong woman. The paint represents something, a symbol of a big and strong woman.

Leila

by Nypri, 11

Once, long ago, there lived a woman who people thought was very strange. She did everything backward. She would dress up in raggedy clothes and go to important places, and people would look at her funny because they were wearing fancy clothes and she was wearing raggedy clothes. She would also hide her face.

But every night at midnight, she would gather all her horses and go in the fields with fancy instead of raggedy clothes and gather stones in a circle and make a fire in the middle of the rocks with leaves in her hair and start dancing with horses.

But she would dance on rocks. It would make her feel stronger and more powerful. She would celebrate herself because she was happy. That's one reason why people thought she was strange. P.S. This story took place in Ethiopia.

Cleopatra's Baby

by Lydia, 9

Hi, I'm Cleopatra's baby.

When I was found with my family many years later, I was parted from all but two of my family. I cried when they were taken away for I'm only six months old. But luckily, I managed to take two of the magic coins they dug up. My mother had told me about them before we were buried thousands of years before! And that if I ever saw them to grab as many as I could.

Since they're as tall as I, I could only get two, the earth and the sky, the two most powerful of them all. The earth 'cause the most living things are on it, and the sky because the moon and sun are in it. So I grabbed them and it made me stay the same age forever. And gave me all the power of the earth and sky. I then grew big and am the most powerful sorceress in the world.

That's all I have to say till another thousands of years pass and I have more to say.

Arama (Meaning Spirit of Life)

by Shaniqua, 16

This artifact is very open. She shows naiveté and sweetness. I think she is young. She is at the age where her breasts are budding and her pelvis and hips are coming out. She has many childbearing years ahead of her. She represents the future and the spirit of her village.

Since she's so open and honest, she probably knows everyone else's problems. She does have a mischievous side. The fact that her feet are pointy suggests she does not work on hard tasks; it shows her femininity and daintiness.

Her arms are stretched out in a surrendering gesture. It shows she's pure, innocent, and free. She isn't restrained. I believe she's seen much, but hasn't been deeply affected by the trials of her village life. Her posture shows she's been thoroughly molded by her childhood.

What makes her who she is is living day by day. She makes the best of her days and wants to be different without being strange or outcast. She wants to follow and live a normal village life, yet she also wants to experience life as a whole.

I feel she's a virgin who has been untouched because her legs were made stuck together. Boys have probably tried to get to her, but she held fast. She was considered very beautiful in her tribe. Not only because of her face, but her inner strength and life. Her mother is proud of her, but prays daily that she might make the right choices.

Her complexion is black, but oddly mixed with her red and brown side. This can show she has many sides or is interested in many things. I'm sure she's been the center of attention many times. She has a wiseness beyond her young years. She will grow old happy. She is one of the prospect youngsters of the village, someone who will have a great future.

She gives her village life, and gives her nationality color and her country spirit. She will be remembered many years after her death, because she is the Arama, spirit of life.

The Story of my Artifact

by Lizzy, 10

I'm going to call my "model" woman Sarabi. Here is the story she tells.

I was born in Africa. My mother took care of all the people in the town. She was what you would call a medicine woman. I was born in a hut, on the plain, by the Great River. I was very sick when I was born. My mother took care of me until I was well. My mother had gotten the disease that I had had. Unfortunately, since she did not have the strength to speak and tell Mistress what to do, my mother died.

So I went and lived with Mistress, who was the "queen" of the village.

My sickness had left me, not deformed, but in a way, different. I could tell things that other people could not. I understood things about the world no one had ever dreamed of. Maybe it was the medicine Mother had given me, but something about me was different, special.

One day, I asked Mistress, "What is more than the Great Number?"

She said to me, "There is NOTHING more than the Great Number, ten, and that is why it is so Great!"

I pondered it, but I did not understand it. There's always something more of something.

I went outside and got one of the gray rocks from the ground. I thought to myself, I can get more than that. So I picked up another rock and put it with the others. See, there is one more than the Great Number.

I did not tell Mistress about my discovery because I thought she might be angry at me for defying the Great Number.

I was almost a grown woman. Tomorrow I would be as old as the Great Number. I had already had my first and second child. Both girls, wonders of nature.

I was the medicine woman of my village. Many had died from the terrible disease, Cuptum. I had many to treat. There were many I could do nothing for. I got the disease.

I would not let my children near me. I did not want them to get sick.

I died one of your "months" after I caught the disease. I felt proud of myself, because I had worked as hard as I could to discover new things that needed discovering. That is why my arms are in such a position.

Remember. Bring everyone into you, to help them, and use your given knowledge to discover what needs discovering.

The stories of the artifacts have given voices to girls and women who might have been lost forever. Each of us has a voice that deserves to be heard, too. That's one of the reasons I chose a strong phrase like "speak out" to describe our girls' program and my book's title. I hope you like it, too.

FINDING YOUR PLACE ON THE PLANET

Today I feel I could take on the world. —*Elizabeth*

ike us, artifacts need homes. Imagine that the floor of the room you're in or the ground you're sitting on is covered with cloth or paper cutouts of the seven continents. It looks like a giant map or a flattened globe. Which continent do you live on? Were your ancestors born on the same continent you were? Can you imagine land bridges between continents thousands and thousands of years ago that people could cross more easily than we can travel between continents today? These land bridges helped one culture absorb the artifacts and customs of distant cultures even before there were motorized ways to travel.

Before the time of written history, many societies on earth were a mixture of different customs and traditions, and these different practices changed them. Some customs and traditions are changing today, which changes the world around us. Changing is a natural part of being alive. For instance, by the year 2040 in the USA, unlike now when the white race is the majority race, there will be no single race in the majority. The citizens of the USA will be multiracial, which means people of different, or multiple, races and ethnicities will participate in the country's democracy. Everything can change, even a five thousand-year-old belief like sexism.

A Place to Stand

Make small- or large-sized continents from paper to place on the floor (they don't have to have each continent's precise shape; as a matter of fact, you can just write the continents' names on pieces of paper). I use large-sized continents that girls made from green fabric in one of the original Girls Speak Out workshops. Trace one of your favorite artifacts in this book, and place your artifact on the continent where you think she would feel most at home. Then just like the girls and women in a workshop, choose a continent to sit on where *you* feel most at home: it can be where you live, where you're descended from, or where you would like to visit or live.

How much do you know about the country or continent your ancestors came from? Are there different shades of skin within one race or a certain feature like an eye shape, for example, that is common to most people on this continent? Do you or your ancestors resemble most of the people from their birthplace? In one workshop, a Chinese-American woman sat on the Asian continent and was surprised to discover that the girl sitting next to her was Japanese-American because the girl didn't look like a typical Japanese-American. They had known each other before but had not talked about their ancestry. Someone can belong to a place even if they look different from the majority of people living in that place. A mix of different races, cultures, and ages appear on each continent when everyone in a workshop is standing on their chosen continent. That's similar to how it is on the actual continents.

Look through your picture collection and decide which girl would live on which continent. Place them there and see how many continents you have populated with females. Step from continent to continent as if you could cross land bridges like our ancestors traveled. Writing positive slogans about girls such as "Girls are great!" on slips of paper and placing them on the continents is fun and creates a vision of a welcoming planet. You are a bridge among girls now.

An Outspoken Woman

Girls of African descent often come from different continents and islands, as do others in this modern world where people move around—sometimes by choice and sometimes not. Many of us know that in the USA some girls' ancestors were stolen from Africa and that, if they survived the journey, they were sold as slaves. During a Girls Speak Out workshop in Chicago, girls talked about what they were studying in black history in Girl Scouts and at the YWCA. They told me they believe the white people they know today are not responsible for the slave trade, but they wonder what people have learned about racism from the last two hundred years of history.

One female ex-slave who tried to educate people about racism, sexism, and classism was named Sojourner Truth. She was given the name Isabella at her birth in 1797, and her last name changed with each new master. She was freed after thirty years as a slave, and in 1843 she changed her name to show the woman she had become: Sojourner, a traveler on a journey who was telling the truth about her experiences as a woman and as a slave. Her audiences weren't used to hearing women speak, especially not a black woman who was a feminist, but Sojourner was a tall, strong woman and a magical speaker who commanded attention.

She was spiritual and would also sing songs at her presentations about her feelings and experiences as if she were in a different kind of church. She joined with the abolitionists, a movement of people who wanted to get rid of slavery. At that time, it was also unusual for a woman to talk about and be active in politics, since women of all races and black men were forbidden to vote and, in many states, even to speak in public.

Tara is a nine-year-old girl in New York, where Sojourner Truth was born, and she shined during a workshop. She asked why there has never been a woman president of the United States. Her companions in the workshop offered explanations, such as the fact that many young women feel that their vote doesn't count even after women fought hard to win the legal right to vote. Women talked about how a patriarchy makes it hard for a woman to be president because we aren't allowed to take the steps to get there or to have the money to run for office. But we said that in the last hundred years or so, a woman's movement has been helping females to become powerful. Today there's even an organization called the White House Project that is helping women prepare, raise money, and campaign for president. Tara carefully listened to each explanation. Then she said in a clear, strong voice, "I'm going to be the first one."

Sojourner Truth couldn't read or write, but she was one of the first women political activists. During the Woman's Rights

Singing Out

If you could change your name to show what you want to do, what new name would you choose? Would you keep all or part of your current name?

One black feminist who's a writer today changed her name to her great-grandmother's name. Instead of Gloria Watkins, she became bell hooks because her great-grandmother "talked back" and bell wants to talk back also—about racism and the patriarchy. bell also uses lower-case letters in her name to indicate that a person's name is not more important than other words. She prefers to use the term "white supremacy" instead of "racism" since the second term could refer to people of color who consider themselves superior, or supreme. White supremacy describes what is really happening to most people of color.

Is there anyone you admire whose name you would adopt? With or without a new name, would you be a speaker, a singer, or a writer? Would you like to be outspoken and a political activist like Sojourner? Fannie Lou Hamer was a black female activist who fought for equal rights for blacks and women in the Civil Rights Movement in the United States. She would sing in defiance of the men who jailed and beat her for speaking out about racism. Her favorite song was called "This Little Light of Mine," and she loved to raise her voice wherever she was and sing, "This little light of mine/ I'm gonna let it shine/ Let it shine/ Let it shine/ Let it shine." Which song do you think expresses your unique inner light?

Convention of 1851, Sojourner gave a speech in which she asked the question, "Ain't I a woman?" She bravely challenged her male audiences (at that time, women were rarely allowed to attend political meetings) to deny that she was as physically strong and intellectually smart as they were.

Another female abolitionist, Frances Dana Gage, wrote down what Sojourner said just the way she said it in what's called "dialect," or folk speech, which is the way a particular person really sounds as opposed to what is changed on the page to make it easier to read. Folk speech is another way of respecting different ways people express themselves. These are the opening lines of what became one of Sojourner's most famous speeches:

> *"Wall, chilren, what dar is so much racket dar must be somethin out o kilter. . . . But what's all dis here talkin bout? Dat man ober dar say dat womin needs to be helped into carriages, and lifted ober ditches, and to hab de best place everywhar."*

You can read the rest of Sojourner's speech in folk speech in *Black Women in America: An Historical Encyclopedia.* In this speech, among other things, Sojourner challenged the audience to remember that slave women and poor women had shown that women were not too weak or too ladylike to be equal, which is what some pro-slavery men were trying to say about women in general, black or white. When Sojourner began to speak, the crowd was angry. The following translation of Sojourner's speech comes from a biography called *Sojourner Truth: Ain't I a Woman* by Patricia C. McKissack and Frederick L. McKissack.

> *"Well, children, where there is so much racket, there must be somethin' out of kilter. . . . The white men will be in a fix pretty soon. But what's all this about anyway?*

"That man over there," she said pointing to a minister who had said a woman's place was to be a mother, wife and companion, good sister and loving niece. Among other things he also said women were the "weaker sex."

To this Sojourner took issue. "He says women need to be helped into carriages and lifted over ditches and to have the best everywhere. Nobody ever helps me into carriages, over mud puddles, or gets me any best places."

And raising herself to her full height, she asked, "And ain't I a woman?"

Sojourner turned to the men who were seated behind her. "Look at me!" She bared her right arm and raised it in the air. The audience gasped as one voice. Her dark arm was muscular, made strong by hard work. "I have ploughed. And I have planted." No doubt she was remembering the years she had worked . . . to earn early freedom. "And I have gathered into barns. And no man could head me." She paused again and asked this time in a whisper. "And ain't I a woman?"

"I have borne [thirteen] children and seen them sold into slavery, and when I cried out in a mother's grief, none heard me but Jesus. And ain't I a woman?" [No doubt Sojourner was thinking about her mother but used "I" instead. Sojourner only had five children.]

Then one by one she took on the male religious pedants. "You say Jesus was a man so that means God favors men over women. Where did your Christ come from?" She asked again. "Where did he come from?" Then she answered her own question. "From God and a woman. Man had nothing to do with him."

She challenged the widely held belief that women were less intelligent than men were, and blacks had no intellect at all. "Suppose a man's mind holds a quart, and woman's don't hold but a pint; if her pint is full, it's as good as a quart." Her common sense *ripped at the core of male hypocrisy.*

Sojourner directed her conclusion to the women in the audience. "If the first woman God ever made was strong enough to turn the world upside down all alone, these women together ought to be able to turn it back and get it right-side up again and now that they are asking to do it, the men better let 'em."

Sojourner's "truth" was simple. Racism and sexism were unacceptable to people of good reason.

My niece lives in northern California, where she acted the part of Sojourner Truth for her middle school drama club. It was such a successful presentation that she was asked to travel to different schools, and she performed Sojourner's and Fannie Lou Hamer's speeches. You can pretend to be a woman you admire, too, and perform for yourself, a few people, or large crowds. Sharing the story and words of an important feminist activist helps people learn what freedoms all people deserve.

The Right to Speak Out

Perhaps you or a girl you know has lost valuable rights, such as the right to speak freely and/or to travel. Some girls in parts of Afghanistan that are controlled by a religious group called the Taliban must keep silent and keep their bodies covered from head to toe. The windows in their rooms are covered, too, to keep them out of sight from passing males. Many girls living under these rules become ill because they suffer from lack of sunlight. I dream that someday girls everywhere will be able to move about freely, make choices, and be healthy.

Each of us must feel safe enough to choose what to say and do. As we speak out, let's hope that girls in places like Afghanistan will hear the whisper of our voices bringing them hope.

Girls' Rights

Sojourner Truth and Fannie Lou Hamer took a lot of chances and said and did a lot of risky things when they were adults. A trusted older friend or adult can help you make a difference and keep you safe. Thinking about why Sojourner tried to change the patriarchal, racist system may give you some ideas about what you'd change today to make life fair for *all girls*.

In the back of this book, you will find a Girls Global Plan of Action that contains a list of specific Girls' Rights. The list was the result of a two-day brainstorming session by girls from eleven countries who attended a girls' conference at the United Nations that Girls Speak Out initiated and helped organize. (The United Nations is a place where about two hundred countries around the world send representatives to promote peace and protect human rights; it began using the phrase "Girls' Rights" in the late 1990s.) Females around the world chose freedom from violence as their most important right. Is it at the top of your list?

Do your own brainstorming. Which Girls' Rights in the back of this book do you think are the most important? Is violence against girls something that you think about? Why or why not? What changes would happen in your life if people respected Girls' Rights? Design a poster or a sign in favor of a Girls' Right. Maybe you can display your poster or sign or explain Girls' Rights to friends, a club, or a class in school.

I hope you enjoy finding your place among girls and women who believe in each other and their right to speak out!

Making Artifacts and Asking Questions

Bring everyone into you, to help them, and use your given knowledge to discover what needs discovering. —*Lizzy*

e have no way of knowing whether or not girls made any of the ancient artifacts in this book, but we can create our own artifacts today. We can use clay, design a collage, or draw and paint one. Our personal artifacts are as unique as we are; they represent us, not images of someone from the past. As a matter of fact, these artifacts move us into the present, even into the future, because they're about Girls Speak Out readers and workshop participants.

If an original girl-made artifact looks like a girl holding a microphone, would you guess that the artist's voice is important to her? Carol in Minnesota made an artifact like this when she was in ninth grade. She's in college now and hosts a program on her school's radio station. Creators value their artifacts when they make them and as they grow older. A seventy-one-year-old woman named Francine was part of the original group who helped

She's Me!

Now is a good time for you to create your own artifact. What kind of artifact would you make to show who you are? Girls have created many artifacts in the workshops, and many have been mailed to me: some have crowns, one held a soccer ball on her fingertips, one showed a young girl sitting with the planet in her lap, there was an infinity symbol, and one featured a notebook with a pen holder. You can draw your artifact in your notebook, you can make a collage that expresses how you feel about who you are, or you can use clay to sculpt it. You may have your own idea about how to create an artifact. The logo or symbol for Girls Speak Out is like an artifact. Her body is the symbol for females, and we added arms to hold a globe. She represents the power of girls everywhere. What do you think?

You can begin by brainstorming what your artifact might look like by listing objects that people can recognize (such as books or footballs) that say something about you. Artists also make abstract images or sculptures; that is, they use shapes that don't look like or represent any object or person. Abstract artists reveal their ideas and feelings with unusual shapes and all kinds of colors. Listening to music and creating abstract shapes with clay can result in an interesting artifact, too. Your artifact is about you, and you are the artist.

What could we guess about you from your artifact? Is there someone you know who you wish knew more about you? Maybe you can ask her or him to guess what your artifact says about you, and as you discuss it, it will help her or him to understand you better.

me create the Girls Speak Out program. Her artifact was handmade from clay because she loved using her hands, preparing food, and making beautiful flower arrangements. Francine was holding her artifact when she died a few years ago, and her husband gave her artifact to me to share with girls.

What I Want to Know

While you are working on your original artifact, will you think of any questions you have for girls and/or women? Girls Speak Out is a place to ask important and personal questions of females of all ages who are not related to you. Is there anything you want to know about growing up? Are there things older girls or women do that energize, anger, or puzzle you? Asking questions can clear up a lot of things and help you decide what you want for your own future.

If you write your questions in your notebook, you might find that you have some of the same issues on your mind as the girls I've met—or you may put something into words that girls on the opposite side of the planet are interested in, too. As you read the questions asked in the next pages, think about something that you would like to talk about with girls and women. Maybe there's a younger girl in your life who would like to ask you a question. If you don't ask or listen, it's harder to learn about something.

Will I Be Me?

Judy is a nine-year-old girl in New York City with huge brown eyes with deep circles under them. Her question for women was, "When did you have children?" It's interesting that she assumed every woman wants to have children. What are your feelings about whether or not a woman should be a mother?

Judy looked surprised as each woman answered her. One by one, we explained our different experiences: I was twenty-six when I had my son; the Haitian woman next to me had two daughters before she was twenty-five; a forty-five-year-old woman from North Carolina said she and her husband chose not to have children; another woman became a mother at thirty-three; and one twenty-one-year-old woman said she wants to have children later on in life, if at all.

Judy then asked why we did or didn't have children. I became pregnant soon after I had cervical cancer, and I wanted to have a baby, in part, because it was a life-affirming event. The Haitian woman said she wanted daughters and was glad when they were born close together so they could keep each other company because she herself had been lonely as a child. The woman who didn't choose to have children said she had an interesting life without children. The remaining two women talked about waiting to share their lives until they felt comfortable taking care of someone for a lifetime.

A young woman then asked Judy if she is interested in having children. Judy told us that her three sisters, who are sixteen, eighteen, and nineteen, already have children, and they live at home with their babies. She doesn't think she wants children, and she can't figure out two things: how to have a family if you don't have kids and how to belong to the "circle of life" if you don't have kids.

In response, one woman said she has a circle, or family, of friends she chooses to be with as well as her children and husband. Two of the women are single parents like me, and we said we think of ourselves as families because a family is any number of people who support and love each other. I even think of myself as a "double parent" because I raised my son without his father's help.

The woman with no birth children explained that she has a lot of friends and nieces and nephews who are part of her family. My friend Gloria is in her seventies, and she's surrounded by young women who are like daughters even though she didn't give birth to children. I have friendships with more and more girls and young women as I get older, and I feel like I have many daughters as well as my actual son.

When I asked Judy why she thinks she has to be a mother to belong to the circle of life, she talked about the movie *The Lion King*, in which there's a song about a circle of life. Judy said she thinks the message in the movie is that having babies is the only way for females to be part of a family and to belong to the human race. She doesn't think boys or men have to be fathers to belong to a family or do anything special to belong to the human race, but she thinks it's unfair that females have to do these things. Judy is describing what is called a "double standard," which is what happens when males follow one set of rules and females have a different and more limiting set of rules. Believing that men belong to our species or to a family just because they were born into it while women have to earn this natural human right is an example of believing in a double standard.

In *The Lion King*, the lion cub's mother is very briefly on screen, and it's because she's given birth to the new lion king. "She's not a lion queen, either," said another girl. Later in the workshop, Judy said she felt better having more choices to think about than the one presented in the movie.

Nicole in Portland, Oregon, wanted to know the age when girls and women in the workshop became interested in boys as boyfriends. One seventeen-year-old girl said she has had a boyfriend for the last few months. They talk on the phone a lot and go out to the movies and to friends' houses, but she feels it's no big deal because she also has other things to do. She wants to be a writer, and getting married isn't on her mind yet. Hally wrote to me after reading Nicole's question to explain that she thinks "people where I live in New Mexico expect a girl to be interested in boys by the time they're eleven or twelve or else they worry 'something is wrong' with her."

In the workshop, when a sixteen-year-old girl said she really, really wants a boyfriend, another girl her age said that girls with boyfriends aren't always as happy as you imagine them to be when you don't have one. How do you feel about her statement? She said she had a steady boyfriend when she was sixteen, but she actually wanted more time to herself. She felt pressure from her boyfriend and from the girls she knew to be a girlfriend.

Nikki is a young woman who was getting married in two weeks. She said that she had been friends with boys when she was a teenager, which is often hard to do without getting romantic. Nikki thought she had a good relationship with her fiancé because they are each other's friends and they also have a romantic relationship.

When a sixteen-year-old girl named Jane said she isn't interested in boys, some of the older girls and women said they felt like that at her age, but their feelings changed. Then a twelve-year-old girl, Kate, spoke about feeling "different" from girls who talk about boys all the time and focus on how much they want a boyfriend. When Jane insisted she likes hanging out with girls better, some of the girls and women in the workshop tried to convince her that she would change, too. Lesbians are females who want to be in a romantic relationship with each other. How do you feel about this kind of single-sex romantic relationship?

Tina, who's thirteen and lives in Harlem, a big African-American community in New York City, said her aunt was a nurse. Tina's aunt explained to Tina that during puberty she would experience many different feelings, including feelings about romantic relationships. Tina told the girls in the workshop, "I could be interested in boys. I could be a lesbian and interested in girls. I could be bisexual and interested in both sexes. Who knows? I'm going to be open-minded about it."

I believe that children in many lesbian families (where the parents are two women in a romantic relationship) and children in male homosexual families (where the parents are two men in a romantic relationship) are very conscious about the importance of positive self-esteem. Part of the reason I believe this is because lesbian and homosexual families are nontraditional families. Many people do not accept the idea of these new kinds of families, and it's even illegal in some places for homosexual parents to marry or adopt children. One result of this lack of acceptance is that these parents often make sure their children understand the value of being different. Girls in the homosexual families I meet learned to believe in themselves and the importance of challenging prejudices at an early age.

Tina, who is in a traditional family, said she feels "connected to everyone and everything on the planet." She knows some kids and grown-ups are upset by bisexuality and homosexuality, but she thinks what people do with their sex life is "none of my business. I just have to figure out who I am." No matter what kind of family we have, each of us can have self-esteem.

Do I Have to Give In to Grow Up?

What parents expect of girls in school is an issue that led fifteen-year-old Cassie to ask the older women in the group if they are close to their parents and sisters and brothers as grown-ups. She said she feels her parents want her to live her life for them—to do the things they missed doing when they were young. Cassie is afraid of disappointing them if she does what *she* wants to do. She told us that even when she is doing something she wants to do—

like doing well in school—if her parents want the same thing, she is unhappy. "That's because," she explained, "if they want me to do it and they don't care what I want, it's like I don't count. I need to do it for me. That's who I am, not just who *they* want me to be."

Two young women who live in San Diego are close in age; they are twenty-three and twenty-five. They look like sisters, but they aren't related. Roz and Minna both said they have a hard time getting along with their mothers, who think they have become "too independent." They aren't interested in marriage, and they both have careers they like—they work with teenagers in high schools—but they don't earn a lot of money.

Roz and Minna live with roommates and enjoy living away from their parents' homes. Each hopes she will get along better with her mother as she gets older. They think part of their problem now is they both are from cultures—Mexican and Filipino—that often believe women should marry young, have children, and give up everything else.

A sixteen-year-old said she can't even mention moving out of the house to her parents. She wants to travel for a year after high school, but her parents explode whenever she tries to bring it up. Other girls said they have older sisters who didn't do what their parents wanted them to do, so they feel it's their turn to give in to make their parents happy. Some girls said they are the oldest or the only child; they feel responsible for fulfilling everyone else's expectations in order to be considered a successful adult.

Roberta is a young woman who was an only child, and she told us her mother encouraged her to do what she liked to do. Her mother was a single parent, and it was hard for her mother to earn enough money to support them and send Roberta away to college. Roberta's mother is a writer now, something she always wanted to be, but she couldn't earn enough money as a writer when Roberta was growing up. Roberta said she now feels free to be who she wants to be too.

Sometimes people have expectations of us that are based on stereotypes, which are mistaken beliefs about *all* the people in a certain group. Stereotypes of girls include beliefs that they aren't as athletic as boys, they have to be thin to be pretty, and they shouldn't act smarter than boys.

Girls tell me that one of the things that happens as they get older is that it's harder to listen to their inner voice because they feel pressured to be like everyone else and not be an individual. By the age of twelve or thirteen, no matter where they live, many girls say they silence their unique voice, and their personalities change when they try to fit in—and this means imitating female stereotypes. Some of them ignore old friends who don't dress fashionably or talk about boys all the time or they tease weaker girls because being mean makes them popular.

The problem is that girls who give up their true selves are unhappy, and many of them are afraid they'll never get their true selves back. I think it's important to know that you, like most girls, can lose your inner voice. You have a better chance of resisting the pressure to conform to stereotypes if you know what could happen to you. Knowing you're at risk of losing your true self is like a warning sign on the highway: it reminds you to slow down and keep your true self safe.

Monica in Australia sent me an email about her choices: "Girls who act like stereotypes and mean girls used to drive me crazy because I couldn't stand how they acted and yet I wanted to be popular, too. Then I realized how awful it is to pretend to be something you're not and to be silly or cruel even if it makes you seem cool. I found a new friend and we feel good about ourselves and have fun together. Now I think we're the lucky ones." When

Stereotypes and Individuality

What do people expect of you because you're a girl? Is there a female stereotype that affects you or someone you care about? How are you or someone else affected by it? Make a checklist comparing what is positive about being an individual and what is positive about being a stereotype. List the problems that individualism (being an individual, true to yourself) and imitating stereotypes raise. Which people in your life support your individuality? Which stereotypes about groups of girls such as teen mothers, fat girls, or anorexic girls have you accepted? How do you feel about rejecting a stereotype if others around you believe it is true?

you feel pressured, stop and check in with yourself, not with the crowd, and remember that there are girls and women like the ones in this book who support you, and you'll feel as good as Monica does.

What if losing touch with yourself has already happened to you? A seventeen-year-old girl in a North Carolina workshop told us, "You can take back whatever you gave up to fit in. Something bad happened to me, and I lost my true self. I want you to know I got it back and I feel great! You can do it, too." True selves are always inside you.

Watch out for stereotypes about *groups* of girls, too. For instance, teen mothers are often stereotyped as losers who can't go to college, have a career, or make good choices. When girls talk about whether or not to have sex, for example, the subject of teen mothers usually comes up, and girls say they're scared of "making the same mistake" as teenage mothers.

Unlikely Friends

Now we're going to read from a novel about a seventeen-year-old teen mother who has left school to work in a factory to support her two children. A fourteen-year-old girl who wants to go to college becomes her babysitter. In *Make Lemonade*, by Virginia Euwer Wolff, when fourteen-year-old LaVaughn sees a note that says BABYSITTER NEEDED BAD it leads her to Jolly, a teenage mother whose children have different, absent fathers. LaVaughn wants to earn money, but she thinks her mother won't like her spending time with Jolly. I'm including the part where LaVaughn explains why she has to babysit, despite the fact that Jolly lives in . . . .

. . . even a worse place than where we live.
The sidewalk is sticky,
the garbage cans don't have lids, somebody without
teeth
was talking to herself in front of the door.

[Because the novel is written as if it were poetry, it looks and often sounds like it has the rhythm of speech. It's easy to read aloud. I encourage you to try reading it aloud.]

This word COLLEGE is in my house,
and you have to walk around it in the rooms
like furniture.
Here's the actual conversation
way back when I'm in 5th grade
and my Mom didn't even have her gray hairs yet.
I'm sitting on the high stool in the kitchen
cutting up carrots and celery. You have to understand

this vegetable work would be a big deal for a little kid
which I was one then.
My Mom was putting the other stew things
together in the pot
and I was thinking about the movie they showed in school.

It was about how you go to college
and the whole place is clean with grass planted
and they have lion statues and flowers growing.
You study in books and do science in a lab with microscopes
and you get to live in the dormitory and make popcorn.
Then you graduate
and you wear a cap and gown and it's outdoors.
Then you get a good job and you live in a nice place
with no gangs writing all over the walls.

I just up and asked her while we doing the stew.
"Can I go to college when I'm big?"
My Mom turns her whole body to look at me
and she stops with the stewpot
and after she looks for a while she says,
"Nobody in this building"—
she waves her arms out sideways with the wooden spoon—
"ever went to college, nobody in my family,"
and she pulling her chin up
and her shoulders and her chest, and she says,
no breath in between,
"somebody got to be the first, right?" And she goes back to the stew.

Nobody in the building? It has 64 apartments.

I used to count the buzzers while I waited
for the squeaky elevator.
In 64 apartments nobody ever went to college.
She told me very clear, so I never forgot it yet
in all these 4 years since,
"You don't get college easy.
College takes 2 things,
money and hard work. And I don't know what else.
I never got there to find out.
Mostly you don't quit what you start.
You stick to the work you begin. You hear me,
LaVaughn?"

I tell her Yes I hear her.
"We don't have college money, LaVaughn. You hear me?"
"Yes."
"You have to earn it. You listening to me?"
"Yes." This was brand-new news to me in fifth grade.
And some other time, maybe that night,
maybe another night,
she was saying good night
and have you done your homework,
and she said, "You go to college, you make me prouder
than I been in my whole life.
That's the truth, LaVaughn, I tell you."

And another time, I don't know when,
she says to me, she's blow-drying her hair to go to work,
she yells, "Listen here, LaVaughn,
what I said about we don't have college money?
You remember?"
I come around the side and yell up in her face
over the blow-dryer,

"Yeah, I remember."
She goes, "Well, we'll have a little bit. A little bit of it.
You earn it mostly, I can put in a little bit. . . ."

That's why that word COLLEGE is in our house
all the time,
it's why I babysit,
it's why I do all the homework all the time,
it's what will get me out of here.
We don't talk about it every day
But it's there.

Even though LaVaughn is poor and lives in a place where no one goes to college, LaVaughn's mother believes that her daughter will be the first one to do it. LaVaughn's and her mother's expectation challenges one stereotype of poor, black girls that says they will drop out of high school and never go to college. An African-American woman from a black community in Kansas told us she grew up seeing black women and men in charge of the businesses in town. Her father owned a gas station. She decided to learn about business, went to college, and graduated with a business degree. She now runs a nationwide program for girls. She learned by observing the positive accomplishments of those around her and rejecting stereotypes about her race and gender.

Sometimes, though, there's no one in a girl's home or community who can be a role model or give her the information she needs. In this situation, stereotypes can seem real because there doesn't seem to be another way to be. My parents thought going to college "wasn't practical" and that I should get a job and marry right after high school. I wasn't happy with that idea; reading and learning excited me so I found out from my favorite teachers how to apply to local colleges. I thought if I lived at home my parents wouldn't try to stop me. It worked, although I would have liked the choice of going away to school or living at home. Sometimes you can't do everything you want, so you choose the main thing.

Sometimes you can find what you want even when you're not looking for it. A forty-eight-year-old woman told us that when she was eight or nine, she used to go to the library every day after school in Queens, New York, because there were no books in her home to read. She would stay until the library closed.

One day, the librarian asked her if she wanted to take the books home, and the girl was shocked. She didn't know that you could take library books into your house. Now she's a literature teacher.

Gloria, who's a writer, found books in her garage to read when she was a girl. Her father used to buy people's books at auctions after they had died. He would sell the valuable books, and put the rest in the garage. She was also taking care of her sick mother, and not going to school, so she went out to the garage and picked up the first book she found. She loved reading and she learned a lot. Now, she thinks that because no one told her what she was supposed to read, she learned early to think for herself. No one told her that some books were for grown-ups, so she read it when she was eight.

Moving Beyond Stereotypes

In *Make Lemonade*, LaVaughn doesn't tell her mother that Jolly's only seventeen because she knows her mom thinks teenage mothers are bad influences—and LaVaughn feels that way, too. As LaVaughn gets to know Jolly and her kids, Jeremy and Jill, however, her ideas about how Jolly got into her situation change:

> *I heard somebody say Jolly didn't face reality.*
> *Jolly she says, "You say that?*

Reality is I got baby puke on my sweater & shoes
and they tell me they'll cut off the electricity
and my kids would have to take a bath in cold water.
And the rent ain't paid like usual.
Reality is my babies only got one thing in the whole
world and that's me and that's the reality.
You say I don't face reality? You say that?"

One day LaVaughn gets angry at Jolly because there are no clean clothes for two-year-old Jeremy. LaVaughn says

"That's the way you did the birth control too?
Part way is good enough?"

Jolly answers

"You carry your schoolbooks
like they're some kind of Bibles,
you go to your classes, you pass your tests,
you smile all pretty at your teachers,
is that gonna make you never get pregnant
some guy gets you down where he wants you?"

It must be scary for Jolly to realize she's responsible for two children and for LaVaughn to hear that violent things could happen to her, but they become friends when they tell each other the truth.

Although their friendship is not easy, LaVaughn continues to babysit when Jolly goes back to school. Near the end of the book, Jolly tells LaVaughn a story she heard at school. It's about a blind woman who buys an orange for her hungry kids. On her way home, some boys trip her and they switch a lemon for the orange. She doesn't realize what they've done, and she thanks the boys for

Friendships and Stereotypes

How do you feel about your ability to make friends? Why is it an easy or complicated process for you? Do you think LaVaughn and Jolly work harder to get to know each other because of stereotypes about a poor black girl going to college or being a teen mother? Do you think *Making Lemonade* is a story about dreams, about friendship, or about stereotypes? Have you ever been angry with someone, then said what you think, and had it bring you closer? Make two lists. One is of Satisfying Friendships and the other is of Shaky Friendships. Do stereotypes affect one or both kinds of friendships? List the ways that stereotyping people affects friendships on either or both lists. Why do you think it takes longer to reveal our true selves in a friendship if we have to consider stereotypes about that friend's looks or family? What can you say to a friend that will reveal more of you? Telling someone something private about you can be risky. If you feel it's risky to tell something, would you tell it anyway? If you actually try this, describe in your notebook what you learned by looking beyond stereotypes.

helping her. LaVaughn says the woman should have figured it was a lemon, and at least "felt it careful."

> *"That's what they always say," [Jolly] says.*
> *"They always say,*
> *'You should've known you was getting a lemon.'"*
> *She exaggerates her voice.*

I begin to get the picture.
"But you don't always know at first," Jolly says.
"You even thank them for it most of the time. See?
See how they get you when you're down,
you don't even know it's a lemon."
She's building up steam, this Jolly is.
"You even thank them for it,
and you go stumblin' home,
all bleeding or however you're hurt—
and you say to yourself,
'Well, gosh, I guess somebody give me a lemon.
Ain't I stupid.
Ain't I dumb. I must've deserved it,
if I was so stupid not to know.'"
And Jolly looks at me,
angry because she understands.

How does the story end? The woman finds "this little teensy bit of old caked, lumpy sugar" and she makes lemonade for her kids.

And I get the point of it this time.

And I want to put my arms all the way around Jolly
in congratulation
and I'm so happy she's so angry
and I'm proud of her
she made it clearer than my mom ever did
with all the preaching and huffing
and bookstraps.

In Jolly's story, the main character uses what she has, even when it's difficult, to make a situation better. No one is blamed if there's a struggle; she just does what she can to improve the circumstances. Isn't it wonderful that Jolly and LaVaughn become friends in such an unexpected way?

In Oregon, when I finished reading this selection, nine-year-old Teresa threw her arms up and said, "I'm so happy." Maybe this story of an unexpected connection between girls who aren't usually friends helped her to understand someone and/or to feel understood, too.

Sometimes it takes time to share our true selves, especially when they're hidden from other people behind a stereotype. A friendship that connects true selves can last a lifetime.

GOING INTO THE WOODS

Sometimes what people say to me can really mean a lot. —Adeola

irls have terrific instincts about whom to trust. They also have their own ideas about what to talk about and when to do it. About halfway through the first workshop, girls often talk about things they haven't shared with anyone before. Some of the girls write or draw something as they listen to others talk about a variety of subjects. I've gathered some of these spontaneous talks together for you because they are proof that good things can happen when you feel it's safe to open up and take risks. I hope you take the time to describe something in your notebook that you think it's time to share.

Eleven-year-old Sarah thinks magic is a part of her life, and she wanted to talk about it right now. Have you ever felt that strongly about something? Have you shared it with others? Sarah said there's "something I can feel, maybe it's fairies, maybe not, but there's something special out there I believe in, yes, I do, I believe in magic." A girl asked Sarah if it is like the feeling during holidays, "the spirit of Christmas." Sarah excitedly agreed with her. When Sarah was talking about whether she believes in magic, even though it is not supposed to be real and she is too old to believe in "stuff like that," everyone was laughing along with her and shaking their heads in agreement. It seems we all believe in magic and the part it plays in our lives.

Twelve-year-old Bertha said she felt something magical happen when she was walking and thinking on the beach near her home. She started dreaming about being a doctor in Mexico and it made her so happy, she said she "felt it wasn't a dream at all, that it was real." She said she'll remember that moment as magic whenever she thinks about who she is. I wonder if you will discover, as I did, that as I grew up and away from being four or five years old, I talked less about magical things even though I still believed magic was in all living things. As a matter of fact, I thought dragons existed until I was in high school. I'm not embarrassed that they're still a vibrant part of my imaginary world.

Sharing Your History

How far back can you remember? What experiences influenced you the most? This could be the beginning of sharing something you have kept inside. Draw or write about your earliest memories, and add more as you grow up, creating your own written history. Include your feelings about magic and magical moments in your notebook. What magical things did you believe when you were a little girl? Which beliefs have stayed with you? Describe or draw a magical moment and include it in your history.

Storytellers

Sierra was nine years old when she came to a Girls Speak Out program in a small town in West Virginia. She said that "history is just what happens. When someone writes it down in a book, they write it from their own agenda. Everyone who has written those books has his or her own agenda. And I don't know if there has ever been a time when men didn't have control."

You may know, as seventeen-year-old Evelyn reminded us, that histories were being told before the patriarchy took over five thousand years ago. Evelyn lives on a Native American reservation in northern Minnesota, and she came to Minneapolis for a program. She said people in her tribe tell each other stories all the time; they're stories that have never been written down, but they're still important.

Evelyn was talking about the *oral tradition* I mentioned in an earlier chapter. She said that stories and history can be passed down from memory by telling them aloud. Special people in tribes were called storytellers, and they listened, learned, and passed the stories onto the next generation—and the stories just kept going for thousands of years. We asked Evelyn to be a Girls Speak Out storyteller, to tell a story about us just as a storyteller would in her tribal gatherings, pretending she knew where each of our mothers was born and something about her life.

Can you be a storyteller for your friends or family? Will you make up an oral history for an imaginary self? Of course, following an oral tradition means telling a story to someone and not just writing it down and having them read it, though you can choose to do that, too. We remember what we hear *and* what we read. Heard or read—whether we listen or follow sign language, see the page or touch Braille—we find ways to learn and remember stories.

One afternoon, I organized a Girls Speak Out reunion in a public housing development in New York City. I thought the girls wanted to meet again to come up with a way to keep Girls Speak Out going on their own. They did have that expectation, and they soon started what they call "Girls' Studies" twice a month. They meet in their apartments and talk about women in history and today's media, and sometimes they read books and ask older women to attend, too.

As we talked at the reunion, I realized they also expected me to tell a story, and I hadn't brought any books with me. Luckily, that morning I had been talking with a terrific oral and written storyteller, Clarissa Pinkola Estés. Clarissa and I were discussing a story in her book, *Women Who Run with the Wolves*, which I thought would be good to tell the girls.

Then Clarissa reminded me, "You have *your own stories* to tell." I knew she was right, and so I'm going to include one of my stories called "Going into the Woods." I can tell it from memory like a storyteller, almost as if I lived it. I used some of my experiences and made up the rest. When I was writing it, I felt as if Sequoia, the girl in the story, was telling it to me. Have you ever had something come to you that feels like it was waiting to flow through you? This story is one of those experiences for me.

I used to live near a redwood forest that I walked in almost every day when I was at home; there's a river running through the middle of the town, which floods almost every winter, and it empties into the Pacific Ocean, just a few miles away. The woods, the river, and the flood in my story come from my experiences living in Guerneville, California. I imagine there are places and events in your life that would be good ingredients in a story.

I was inspired by girls I know to write my own story. I hope the story of a girl named Sequoia who goes into the woods and discovers what it means to be free inspires you to create your own unique story that you'll tell to someone. The stories that we carry inside us, that we create, are as important as the ones we find in books.

Once there was a girl who lived with her people in a place where giant trees grow, trees that are so tall they catch the rain just as it leaves the clouds. It's often very dark where these trees grow because they block the sun, and the girl's people don't go into the woods. They call it "The Dark Place."

The girl's name is Sequoia, she's nine years old, and she lives just a short walk from the dark place. All her life Sequoia wanted to go into the woods. She believed she would be where she wanted most in her life to be, a place where someone would listen to her and know that she had feelings, too. It seemed to her that as hard as they tried, the people she knew, including her parents, just didn't think she was as special as a boy. Inside, Sequoia felt as tall as the trees in the dark place. She knew they were special, too, and she felt sad that she couldn't go into the woods.

Each winter, when it rained, sometimes as much as two feet in one day, the river in town would rise up, and come close to the edge of the dark place. Sequoia heard her grandfather say that even the water was afraid to go into the woods. Everyone was quiet when he said that. Sequoia wanted to disagree with him, but she had been told not to say what she was thinking out loud if it would cause trouble. There were a lot of things she didn't say, but she thought often about a moment when she would say what she was thinking about the dark place—and some other things, too, that she had on her mind.

Sequoia was what her mother called a "water baby." She had learned to swim in the river when she was small enough to be held in two hands, and she couldn't remember ever feeling scared of the water. To her it seemed as big and welcoming as the giant trees. It had an everywhere kind of feeling, like the joy she felt sometimes when she watched the sun touch her kitten's head and everything seemed to come together. During a flood, she watched the river to see how far it would dare to go, breaking all the rules her people set for it.

The winter I'm talking about, it rained two feet in ten hours and it kept on raining. It was Sequoia's birthday, and she spent the day watching the rain fall. She went outside to help her mother dig a ditch where the water could run off away from their house in case the creek behind her house rose so fast that there was what they called a "flash flood." Then the water from behind the house could come up so fast—in a flash—that everything in its way would be swept into the river and carried to the mouth of the river where it empties into the ocean.

There was a flash flood that day at a friend's house, and almost everyone ran there to dig ditches. Then they stayed to help clean up and reclaim things of theirs that had been swept into the friend's backyard.

Sequoia stayed at home, and she decided that she would dig a ditch from her bedroom to the dark place. She hoped that the water would rise, take her into the woods, and there she could say everything she wanted to say, out loud, in the place where it was okay to be herself. She dug behind the house, and as the afternoon was turning into night, she realized that she was so strong that she would make it to the edge of the woods and be home in time for the evening meal.

Her parents were coming down the path, covered with silt from the river, and they said they had to go back after getting some food because there were flash floods all over town. It was still raining.

Sequoia wasn't feeling disappointed about missing her birthday celebration because she had plans, too. She promised her parents she would be safe, and they left after throwing together some food and gathering up some dry clothes.

Sequoia's ditches were filling with water. She connected them to the ditch running alongside the path, and then she crossed her fingers that so much water would come that she would float into the woods. She was soon rewarded. The water rose quickly and before she could think twice, she was on her way into the woods.

When she finally was able to stand up, she saw she would have been in total darkness if it wasn't for the full moon sneaking here and there among the treetops. The blackness felt good. And there was something strange happening, too. It wasn't raining under the trees. There was a canopy of branches above her head that shielded her. The trees were covering her. She walked over to one giant tree and felt its bark. It came away in her hands in scratchy pieces and when the moon shone on the bark, she saw it was reddish-brown in color.

"Why, you have red wood," she said to the tree. "Your color is like my skin color. I knew we were from the same place."

Sequoia walked through some of the trees with holes so big that they were like tunnels. She talked with a jackrabbit and a doe playing on the opposite side of the creek. She talked about feeling strong, as strong as anyone she knew, and she told the trees that she was as tall inside as they were. They didn't seem to mind. She thought they liked having her company.

When she wandered back to the edge of the woods, she noticed she had made a path in the twigs, branches, and ferns covering the ground. And she heard voices calling out, "Sequoia."

"They're calling you, too," she said to the tall trees. "We are the same, aren't we? And with you, I see how powerful I am and how powerful everything is. I'm telling my people that I'm coming back into the woods. Maybe they'll come, too. No matter what, I'll be back."

Sequoia walked to the edge of the woods, and she saw her grandfather trembling with anger.

She called to him, "Grandfather, you're wrong about the woods." She walked up to him and said, in a gentle voice that soothed him, "Maybe some day you'll understand, if you listen to what I have to say. After all, I have been in the dark place, and I can tell you what I feel. It's my special place."

Sequoia was right. She did come back to the place where she could be herself, sometimes by walking into the redwoods and sometimes by quietly visiting her place inside herself where she was also protected from the rain and was safe in the darkness.

Girls are usually quiet after a story, especially one about a young girl alone in the woods. Lin, a nine-year-old girl at the Girls Speak Out reunion, leaned forward in her chair, and I could see she wanted to ask a question. She had been silent during our earlier meetings, and now everyone waited for her to speak.

Lin sat up straight and asked, "Why do we go into the woods?"

I said, "I think it's because in the woods we find bad and good, joy and sorrow, love, fear, and hope—and life. Unless you take a risk, you can't find your strength."

Lin thought for a moment and then she said, "Oh, I didn't know that, but that's it. That's what life is about."

A month later, Laurie, a sixteen-year-old, asked a different question at a different workshop. Laurie told us at the opening of the workshop that she was born when her mother was fifteen. Now, she and her mother live with her grandmother. Laurie is upset because her grandmother tells her and her mother what to do. Laurie says her mother isn't independent anymore, and her mother wants Laurie to stay home, not date until she is older, and not go away to college.

Laurie told us, "My mother went into the woods when she had me, then she left the woods when I was born to go back home and live her mother's life. What can I do?"

I said, "You have your life to live. I think you're considering going into the woods. That's your choice. I think your mother makes her own choices that are independent and separate from your choices. Remember, you may be surprised by your family's reactions, and you may surprise yourself. No one, not even you, knows what kind of joy there will be in your future."

I think about these conversations often. I also think that Sequoia's feelings for the woods are like the magic or fairies Sarah talked about. Both are probably our own true selves and best instincts looking after us.

Now you can understand why I've included so many girls' and women's stories in this book. Each of us has unique stories to tell. We all need someone who listens to us and encourages us to share our true selves.

Check In Giving Advice

How do you feel about my conversations with Laurie and Lin? What would you have said to them? What advice have you given to someone? How was it received? What advice haven't you shared that you think might be valuable? Why don't you write it in your notebook? It might be valuable in the future, too. What advice do you have for your parents about raising a daughter or a son?

How do you feel about going into the woods and being on your own? What advice would you give yourself? After all, you know yourself the best.

The Green Stone

My true self just woke up from a loooonnngggg catnap. —*Lydia*

re you ready to move from the time of ancient artifacts into the present and the future? It's time for girls to take center stage. Girls produce and perform in a talk show during the second workshop. In order for that to happen, the girls make plans by themselves at the end of the first workshop. The first and one of the most important choices they have to make is the topic of the talk show.

After we choose a talk show topic, it's time to come together for our last story of the first workshop—and our first picture book. The story is *Finding the Green Stone* written by Alice Walker and illustrated with colorful paintings by Catherine Deeter. Right now, I'm looking at an original painting from the book. It's hanging on the wall next to me. The painting reminds me that we can use pictures to express our emotions and ideas. There's definitely a story in each of Catherine's paintings and in the face of each of the

Girls Seen and Heard

You can make your talk show topic choice now, too. Most of the time, the talk show topics the girls choose have to do with their bodies. What topic about a girl's body would you suggest for a talk show? Is it about size, clothes, or self-image? Now is a good time to prepare yourself as an expert on your topic. Remember the Girls Speak Out collection of pictures you made in one of the first Check Ins in this book? You can add even more diversity to your collection by finding pictures of healthy girls, including girls who aren't unhealthily thin like many models in the media. These pictures may be harder to find because most published images of girls' bodies are of thin and sedentary (posed being still) girls. You might include pictures of girls who are doing something physical like climbing a tree or playing sports in your collection. Girls who look happy with different size bodies would make interesting additions. Your collection could be used to educate other girls interested in running a talk show; the variety of body sizes in your collections will challenge female stereotypes and will stimulate valuable discussions.

people in them. If you go to a bookstore or a library, I know you will enjoy looking at them.

Alice is known to many girls because her book *The Color Purple* was also made into a popular movie and a musical play. Alice says some of her stories, like *Finding the Green Stone*, come to her in her dreams. Reading Alice's book at this point in our day—it's nearly three o'clock; we're tired and are stretched out on the floor, some of us on our stomachs, some cross-legged, and some sitting up or leaning against a friend—helps us relax. How are you resting? This story catches us in an almost dreamlike state. When you are comfortable, have a snack and settle in because it's time to find out about green stones.

Remember when I mentioned earlier that we've re-created our past with the ancient artifacts, and that once we had given the artifacts voices in the present, we would move into the future? We're doing it now. One of the great things about moving into the future with Alice's story is that it tells us about another way to connect from the inside out with the people around us. As a matter of fact, it's about a way to connect with everyone.

I always read *Finding the Green Stone* in a workshop, and I'm so glad you can share it, too. I've shared this picture book with girls and boys from eight to eighteen years old. Each time I understand something new about it and all of us. What stays the same is that readers and listeners sit almost without breathing as the search for something valuable unfolds, and we understand something about ourselves. Each person is separate and thoughtful.

Reading *Finding the Green Stone* alone as you are probably doing is just as powerful as reading it aloud or listening to other people read it. For me, no matter where I am or whom I'm with, it's what happens inside me that stays with me and inspires me. It's the message, not how it's delivered, that moves me. I wonder if you will feel the same way.

As you read, look for clues about differences between Johnny's and Katie's characters.

> *Right at this very time, in a small community on the Earth, live a brother and sister who have identical, iridescent green stones. The stones shine brightly and are small enough to fit into their hands. The children prize their stones and often play with them, taking them out of their pockets and holding them up to the sun, putting*

them in the clear water of the seaside among the rocks and plucking them out again, and so on. They are very happy with their stones.

But one day Johnny, the brother, lost his green stone. He looked everywhere for it.

Then he looked at his sister Katie's green stone, and, because his own stone was missing, he imagined that hers looked bigger and shinier than ever. He thought maybe his green stone had disappeared into hers.

"You've stolen my green stone!" he said.

"No way!" said Katie.

Johnny frowned at her and tried to grab her green stone—and even the memory of his own green stone vanished.

As the days passed, Johnny became very dull and sat for hours under the big tree in the center of the community.

But Katie never forgot that Johnny had once possessed his very own brightly glowing green stone, exactly like hers. And every day, while he sat under the tree fuming and casting mean looks at everybody who passed and sometimes muttering nasty things as well, she brought him her green stone to hold and reminded him that he had once had one, too.

At first, Johnny liked to play with Katie's stone, because whenever he did so he felt much better. But then he would remember that it was hers and that he did not have one of his own, and he would become angry.

One day, when Johnny was feeling this way, he tried to steal Katie's stone by pretending it was his.

"This is my green stone," he cried, clutching it in his fist, not intending to give it back, "not yours!"

But as soon as he did that, the stone turned gray in his hand, just like the rocks by the ocean, and when he looked over at Katie again she had her green stone, as bright and shining as ever!

Tricks or Trust?

At this point, we often pause in the reading to figure out what we might do. What would you say to Johnny? Would you trust him or do you feel more loyal to Katie? Ten-year-old Alicia said she definitely wouldn't help her brother because he plays tricks on her and picks on her all the time. Each thing we do or don't do has a consequence. That's certainly true for Johnny and Katie right now. Let's see what Katie does and how Johnny and Katie react.

Johnny felt sad. He realized that stealing somebody else's green stone would never make it his. Besides, it was lonely under the big tree, and trying to look mean all day was boring.

One day he mustered the courage to talk about his change of heart to Katie, who rarely talked to him now because she was afraid.

"I will never try to steal your green stone again," he said to her. "But I miss my own stone so much. Will you help me find it?"

At first Katie didn't know what to do. How could she believe Johnny meant what he said? That he would not try to grab her green stone?

"No," she said, after a long pause. "I can't help you at all."

Johnny's eyes were bright with unshed tears. Katie could see he meant her no harm, but something inside her liked being the powerful one for a change.

"No," she said again, sticking out her chest just as she'd seen Johnny do. But when she said "No" the second time, with a new coldness in her heart, her own green stone began to flicker and almost stopped shining!

Katie glanced at Johnny's sweet, sad face, so like her own, and then at her flickering green stone. Being spiteful to her brother would never work.

"I love you, Johnny," she said quietly. "I'm happiest when you have your very own green stone. I will do everything I can to help you find it."

The radiance of her stone, when she said this and reached for Johnny's hand, dazzled them both.

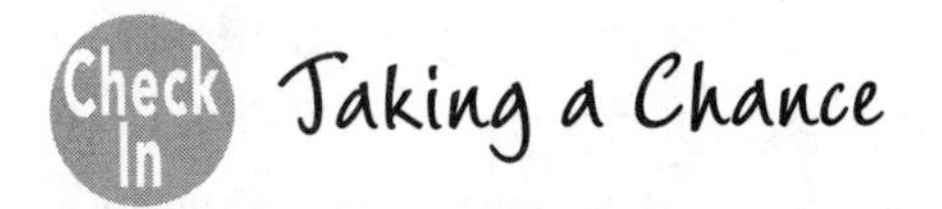

Check In: Taking a Chance

When Katie agrees to help, Alicia cried out, "No, she betrayed me!" How do you feel about Katie's decision and Alicia's reaction? How do you describe the different things that happened to Katie's stone as a result of her choices? Maybe Katie and Johnny have some things in common. List what you think they have in common.

In their search for the green stone, Johnny and Katie ask for help from neighbors and their parents. Johnny was mean to most of these people when he was sitting under the tree, and he's ashamed to ask for help. But when his father and next-door neighbor realize that Johnny is really suffering, they agree to join the search for his green stone. Have you noticed any other differences between Katie and Johnny besides how they treat people? How powerful do you think each of them feels at this point?

Johnny's mother, who's busy as the town doctor, says:

"Listen, son, everybody has his or her green stone. You ought to know that by now. Nobody can give it to you and nobody can

take it away. Only you can misplace or lose it. If you've lost it, it's your own fault. . . .

"We will get everybody in the community to help look for your green stone anyway."

But the search isn't successful. When everyone finally stops to rest under the big tree whose ". . . green stone was one of its millions of fat green leaves," Johnny picks up a rock and he's feeling sad.

He was not crying just because he'd lost the green stone; he knew that because of his hurtful behavior, he deserved to lose it. He was crying because all these people, and especially Katie, loved him and were trying to help him find his green stone, even though they knew perfectly well he could only find it for himself!

He was puzzled that everyone in his community wanted to help him do something he could only do himself, and in his puzzlement, he began to feel as if a giant bee were buzzing in his chest. It felt exactly as if all the warmth inside himself was trying to rush out to people around him. . . .

Katie explains to Johnny why everyone helped him search for something only he could find.

"We wanted to be with you when you found it!" said Katie, softly, wiping Johnny's tears away with her sleeve.

And sure enough, when Johnny followed Katie's gaze and looked down at his hand, what did he see? Not the dull and lifeless rock that he'd thought he was holding, but his very own bright green stone!

. . . (All the people) welcomed the rising of a bright green sun in his heart, which they knew was Johnny's love for them, its warm light overflowing the small brown fingers clutched close to his chest.

At the end of the picture book, there are no words. Catherine Deeter's paintings show everyone dancing around a tree, as if seen from the sky, and the tree is like a green stone. The next painting shows the whole continent, which also echoes the green stone. And the last painting shows the Earth, like a green stone floating in the universe, because the unique and special place inside each of us is a small version of the universe outside.

Now is the time to share green stones, which are smooth, shiny, and small enough to fit into the palm of your hand. I've given pictures of green stones and actual green glass stones to thousands of girls and women. Sometimes I couldn't give girls green glass stones in a workshop because they were in a jail or juvenile detention center, and it was against the rules. They told me that drawing or painting a green stone is a good alternative because it captures the spirit and message behind the green stone. Often it isn't what we touch, but what we feel inside that's worth holding onto.

Each of us can imagine a beautiful green stone glowing with a soft light inside us. It is a place inside where you can go, and no one can follow you, no one can hurt you, and no one can change you. Every human being has this unique place. The green stone is only a symbol to remind us of this special place.

In this story Katie and Johnny each have a green stone that symbolizes her or his own inner self. Each living thing has a special spirit that glows like a green stone. It's important to remember that boys, too, have a unique self that can shine just like Johnny's green stone.

Green Stones and True Selves

What list of words describe Katie's green stone? Johnny's green stone? Which words do Katie and Johnny share on each list? Why do you think each person in their community has a green stone—and why are they identical on the outside, even though each one belongs to only one person? And remember, the tree, the continents, and the Earth are green stones, too. Draw or paint a picture of your green stone and fill it with words that reveal what you feel about connections between people and the Earth. Decorating words such as love and joy with hearts and rainbows and using arrows and clouds to illuminate hate and sadness is another way to express your feelings.

Express your vision of being connected to other people or the planet in an abstract picture. If you want to think about experiences that make you feel isolated or disconnected, sketch or write those, too.

Now's the time to begin thinking about who your true self is because you're going to be asked to write about it in a little while—and to read what other girls have written about their true selves.

Twelve-year-old Kitty in Texas said that even though she could write about a lot of different feelings, her true self was composed of two main ingredients, kindness and humor. Miranda said her green stone was "feeling," the power to feel. "People need to remember," she said, "that all girls have feelings."

During the week that follows the first workshop, I ask the girls to be their true selves, and to think about what they can do to continually tap the power of that self. You can keep a diary in your notebook to record when your powerful true self emerges. If you write things down, you can look back at different times in your life and be reminded of the power of your inner life. Maybe you'll surprise yourself because I'm sure you'll find you have leadership skills that can help you be who you want to be.

The Tunnels Game

Before you take a stretch break, I want to tell you about a ritual game, something we do at the end of each workshop that is fun. Girls who are reading and girls in workshops really enjoy moving around. One person by herself can do some of the movements in the game described below.

I call the game Tunnels and it has become a "rite of passage," which is an experience that marks a turning point in our lives. Tunnels is simple and fun to play: First, the women stand in pairs, facing each other, with their hands stretched overhead forming a tunnel. (There can be a three-person hookup if there's an extra woman.) The girls line up at one end of the tunnel made by the women, with plenty of clearance at the opposite end because the girls are going to run through the tunnel one at a time. They enjoy trying to be fast, and to make it to the end of the tunnel without being tickled.

After stretching your arms as far up as you can, you can run in place weaving and dodging your upper body from left to right as girls do in a workshop. Twirling in a circle also expresses some of the energy that comes from being connected to our bodies.

Then it's the girls' turn to let the women pass through their tunnel. If I'm lucky, I go first, before the girls have a chance to think of more and more ways to surprise (and tickle) the women as they run through. It's as if each group is giving the other group permission to go on to future adventures, almost like giving birth to each other. You can celebrate, too, reaching for the sky and bending to touch the ground as you make a circle with your arms above your head.

We're laughing and hugging as we leave. Hugging yourself is a pretty good idea, too. It can be a reminder that your green stone is deep inside where only you can go.

Together Again

You have to love yourself before you can love anyone else. —Keosha

n my way to a YWCA for the second workshop of a Girls Speak Out program in South Carolina, I heard some-one excitedly calling my name. I turned around to see nine-year-old Anna come running to meet me in the door-way. When she caught my eye, she started waving her hand with a green stone in it, yelling, "My green stone was shining all week! My green stone was shining all week!" I remember this with tears in my eyes, the kind of tears that mean you're really happy.

At the first workshop, Anna had come with a group of girls who had been removed from their homes for their own safety—to be protected from abusive or neglectful parents—and they were living together in a special group home. One of the counselors who traveled with them had told me that Anna was depressed a lot and she might try to run away. When I had told Anna what the counselor had said, I also told her I would like her to stay with the other girls for both workshops and not leave at the beginning of our first day together. Anna had looked at me and said, "If I wanted to run away, I'd be gone by now because there are open doors all over this place."

Anna did stay. But when her counselor saw one of the other participants with a camera, the counselor told Anna that she couldn't have her picture taken because she was being hidden from her father who had sexually abused her. So Anna had gone on strike and didn't talk for most of the day. Can you empathize with Anna; that is, can you put yourself in Anna's place? How does empathizing help you understand her silent strike?

As the day went on, and more pictures were taken, Anna had ducked behind a small blackboard that was resting on the floor. She had drawn two arms, two legs, a neck, and a head with chalk. She had pretended the figure she drew was her body and that we could photograph it. She was pleased when we took a picture of her drawing because she had protected herself in case the picture was seen by her abusive father *and* she had found a way to be included.

While *Finding the Green Stone* was being read, Anna had sat on a ledge next to me and drew. When I had finished reading the story, she had turned her pad around and showed us that it said "FEMALE" in very intricately decorated letters. She then had taken the video camera we were using and filmed everyone as she asked them whether they were coming back the next week. Her counselor had told me she usually didn't appear interested in anything for more than a few minutes, and she was surprised Anna had stayed with us all day, and was still talking and joking with us.

During the week, Anna's mother had sent Anna pictures of herself that she had put on display. Her green stone had a special place on the table next to her bed, alongside a photograph of herself when she was a baby.

Sometimes when someone is angry, and as hurt and sad as Anna feels, I don't know what to do. Now I understand that girls in Anna's situation have their own ways of listening. I am able to empathize with them. I know, too, that their true selves are like the girl flying across the parking lot, happy to be who she is and running into the room for another series of Girls Speak Out adventures.

New Directions

Girls and women who have attended the first and second Girls Speak Out workshops tell me that they remember them as exciting and happy times, but the talk in the second workshop can be more private. As in the first workshop, it's confidential just like your notebook.

If you think of this page as a rectangular room, picture the first workshop with an empty space in the center of the room, and each corner holds four or five girls and women. In one city, the groups separated into the corners were different races and cultures: African-American girls in one corner, white girls in another, Latina girls and Vietnamese girls in the other two corners.

In the second workshop, picture the center of the room filled with girls of different races, cultures, classes, and abilities. They're standing and laughing and talking together. Instead of keeping a distance from people who don't look like them, by the second workshop, girls are enjoying each other as individuals.

What do you think they're talking about? I've heard conversations about where their green stones are, who lost theirs and who kept theirs, and who remembered to bring them to the second workshop. Most of the girls have theirs with them, and some have brought the stones in holders they've made or improvised. Sometimes the stones are in a drawstring pouch on a ribbon around a girl's neck, the kind of pouch that holds a treasure you don't want to lose, and sometimes they're tied in fabric and hanging from a belt loop on a girl's jeans. Pictures of stones have been kept in purses, pockets, and lockets.

Who's in Charge? Game

If you think we play a game at the start of the second workshop, you're right. It is another ritual I like to follow—we do the clapping game you read about before for as long as the girls want to, especially if there's anyone new in the room There's also a new game to learn called Who's in Charge?

Who's in Charge? begins when everyone is seated. One girl volunteers to leave the room, and we ask her not to listen to what's going on inside while she's outside. When she's gone, I explain that one girl in the room will be the leader, doing something like clapping her hands on her knees or tapping her shoulders. The rest of us have to imitate what she's doing, but we can't stare at her because the girl who's outside the room is coming in to guess who's in charge. We don't want to make it too easy.

You can practice changing movements quickly or slowly. Clap slowly, then switch to touching your shoulders, then touch your nose. You can speed this sequence up and then slow it down to exercise your upper body or jog in place to exercise more of your your whole body. Once the volunteer comes back in, she has three guesses as to who's in charge. When she's done, whether she's guessed right or not, it's someone else's turn to be the leader. The old leader leaves the room, and the girl who just guessed (or tried to guess) the leader chooses the new leader. It's challenging to switch movements when you're leading and to avoid looking at the leader.

Remember the clapping game from the first workshop? The same thing that happened there happens here. Remember what it

You're a Leader

Reading stories and leading spontaneous talks, such as the one about magic described in a preceding chapter, are opportunities for girls in workshops to take charge and practice being leaders. Girls make excellent leaders. I enjoy sharing stories of girls taking charge with you, because you, too, are a new leader. Have you been a leader in sports, in academics, or socially? What and whom would you like to lead in the future?

One theory is that a good leader leaves no followers behind because she teaches everyone else to be leaders, too. What do you want to teach people about girls? Have you considered organizing a lunchtime discussion group or forming a weekend or after-school club to publicize ideas about girls as leaders? Boys who support your goals can join, too, as long as the girls feel comfortable in a coed group. What are some of the activities these members could undertake? A teenager in England named Margaret started a Girls Speak Out Club, and the girls circulated a petition to have playing time on the soccer field that was equal to the time allocated to the boys' team. What is a good name for a group about girls' leadership? Create a mission statement—that is, a brief description of the group's goals—in no more than three or four sentences.

was? Girls may change the rules. For Who's in Charge?, one of the "old" leaders can be a leader twice because no one expects it to be the same girl. Sometimes we've also decided that no one will be in charge, so we plan what activities we'll do and the order in which we'll do them, with no actual leader. Doing things randomly without a leader is really a lot of fun. It requires a different kind of concentration, and it gives the person who's outside the room something new to guess.

What's next? If you guessed food and/or a story, you're right. Juice, water, fruit, and/or muffins, maybe sweet bread, are the usual choices. By this time in the program, a girl will read some or all of a story of her choice, perhaps she and I will take turns reading, or two girls may read together, especially if there's a conversation in the story.

A New Family

The story we begin the second workshop with comes from a novel named after its heroine, *Ellen Foster*. Eleven-year-old Ellen is an unexpected leader and an unusual heroine. She's a very independent, very poor white girl from a family in the American South. Both her parents neglect her, and her father sexually abuses her. Ellen has grown up with bad feelings about her own social and economic class and with feelings of superiority because she's white, and these feelings confuse her. In particular, she battles with her prejudices against a black girl, Starletta. One of the amazing things about Ellen is that even when she's struggling and doesn't like herself, she keeps her sense of humor. While she's determined to get what she wants, she doesn't take herself so seriously that she can't laugh at herself and at her mistakes.

Ellen Foster is Kaye Gibbons's first book, and Kaye lives in the southern part of the USA, too, in North Carolina. Kaye wrote *Ellen Foster* in six weeks, and she says it was as if she was just talking out loud to the paper. At the beginning of the book, Ellen is pretty much alone in the world.

As the novel opens, Ellen begins with a surprising description of how she feels about her parents. One of the unique things about

Ellen is that she doesn't feel guilty about having angry feelings about her parents, who treat her badly:

> *When I was little I would think of ways to kill my daddy. I would figure out this or that way and run it down through my head until it got easy.*
>
> *The way I liked best was letting go a poisonous spider in his bed. It would bite him and he'd be dead and swollen up and I would shudder to find him so. . . .*
>
> *But I did not kill my daddy. He drank his own self to death the year after the county moved me out. I heard how they found him shut up dead in the house and everything. Next thing I know he's in the ground and the house is rented out to a family of four.*
>
> *All I did was wish him dead real hard every now and then. And I can say for a fact that I am better off now than when he was alive. . . .*
>
> *Oh but I do remember when I was scared. Everything was so wrong like somebody had knocked something loose and my family was shaking itself to death. Some wild ride broke and the one in charge strolled off and let us spin and shake and fly off the rail. And they both died tired of the wild spinning and wore out and sick. Now you tell me if that is not a fine style to die in. She sick and he drunk with the moving. They finally gave in to the motion and let the wind take them from here to there.*

Before she was taken out of her house and before her father died, Ellen's mother had died, and Ellen was left alone at home with her father. At her mother's funeral, Ellen says:

> *. . . My daddy wonders if I plan to tell somebody the whole story. I do not know if there is a written down rule against what he did but if it is not a crime it must be a sin. It is one way or the other. And he wants to know if I'm telling.*

One day at school, Ellen's teacher notices a bruise on Ellen's arm. Ellen tells her teacher that her father is sexually abusing her and calls what he does "the squeeze." Her teacher arranges for Ellen to live with another family. Ellen goes from family to family until she sees a woman who has lots of foster kids (Ellen takes the word Foster as her new last name). Ellen decides she wants to live with them—and she does. She moves in with the family in the brick house where the school bus stops.

As *Ellen Foster* ends, there is still one person in Ellen's life to whom Ellen wants to say something important—it's her African-American friend Starletta. Despite what was happening in Ellen's life, and despite the fact that having white friends is dangerous in their community, Starletta and her family took Ellen in, listened to her, and helped her feel secure. Ellen invites Starletta to spend the night in her new home because she is trying to find a way to thank Starletta and she wants to overcome her own racial prejudices.

> *Starletta, I've looked forward to you coming to my house and I hope you have a fine time here. I sure like it here. Do you remember me living with my daddy and how I used to come to your house so much?*
>
> *I sure do she says to me and it takes twice as long for her to get that out as normal because she stutters bad and she gets frustrated.*
>
> *Well I came to your house so much because I did not want to be with my daddy and mostly because I like you so much. Even if my daddy was the president I would have still run down to your house whenever I needed to play. Do you believe me?*
>
> *And I look at her so she can nod and will not need to speak. She hates to talk.*
>
> *Starletta, I always thought I was special because I was white and when I thought about you being colored I said to myself it sure*

is a shame Starletta's colored. I sure would hate to be that way . . . the three of you live in that house that's bout to fall down. I always went away from your house wondering how you stood to live without an inside toilet. I know your daddy just put one in but you went a long time without one. Longer than any white folks I know. And when I thought about you I always felt glad for myself. And I don't know why. I really don't. And I just wanted to tell you that. You don't have to say anything back. You just lay there and wait for supper.

And I will lay here too and wait for supper beside a girl that every rule in the book says I should not have in my house much less laid still and sleeping by me.

But while I watch her sleep now I remember they changed that rule. So it does not make any sense for me to feel like I'm breaking the law.

Nobody but a handful of folks I know pays attention to rules about how you treat somebody anyway. . . .

I came a long way to get here but when you think about it real hard you will see that old Starletta came even farther. . . .

And all this time I thought I had the hardest row to hoe.

That will always amaze me.

The room is usually very quiet for a while after this story. Anita, a nine-year-old girl in San Jose, California, had a strong reaction. She burst out and said, "Girls have something men want. Men aren't going to get it. Men and boys have nothing exciting happening to them so they try to take it from us." Anita was in a special program for girls who had been abused by family members, and she wanted us to know that no matter what, she is a valuable person.

Anita and Ellen are both talking about things that usually aren't talked about by or with young girls, things like neglect, poverty, sexual abuse, physical abuse, verbal abuse, incest, and racial bias. What amazes me is that while these difficult things can happen to girls, people pretend they don't. Girls have a hard time when bad things like this happen to them. Being alone as Ellen was at first makes it harder for a girl to know she should not be treated this way. And having no information about these types of things, such as it's not the fault of the victim, adds to that sense of being all alone.

What happened to Ellen, she learns, is against the law, and it happens to some little boys, too. Ellen found people who helped her get out of a bad situation. She didn't feel or act isolated anymore.

Telling, like Ellen did to a teacher she trusted, can be very hard, but it's often the only way other people can know what's happening to children, especially when it's family members or friends who betray a child's trust in them. Girls tell me that telling someone they trust, who believes them, makes a big difference in their lives. One of the reasons I started Girls Speak Out is to give this kind of information to girls so they know it's not their fault if something bad happens to them. Like Ellen, my father sexually abused me when I was young, but I didn't remember what had happened until I was in my forties. When I was young, I didn't know that girls could tell someone they trust what has happened to them, or that girls can survive and heal a deep wound like this one. I'm especially proud that Girls Speak Out is a place to talk and write about things that aren't usually mentioned in other places. Your notebook is one of those places, too.

A New Name

Five years ago, when she was fourteen, my niece spent the night at her best friend's house. She fell asleep on the living room floor, and the other girls were in the bedroom. Yulahlia woke up during the night, and her friend's father was undressing her. He raped her.

His six-year-old daughter was asleep on the couch so my niece didn't make any noise because she didn't want the girl to wake up and be frightened by what her father was doing. Yulahlia didn't tell anyone. She went home in the morning and took a shower.

A month later, Yulahlia told her boyfriend and he told her father. When I found out, I took her to a doctor to make sure she was tested for AIDS and other diseases. She was physically healthy. My niece is part Puerto Rican, and we lived in a mostly white community. After talking to lawyers and judges, we decided that it would be almost impossible to get a fair trial, both because of racial prejudice, and because my niece hadn't told right away while there was still evidence of rape.

I found a woman therapist who works with young girls who are survivors of rape. My niece was in counseling until she went away to college. She's the only one of her friends to go to college, and she's proud she got a scholarship and did all the applying herself.

When we were unpacking her clothes and stuffed animals in her dorm room right before school began, my niece told me she wanted to change her name. She explained, "I'm a new person here. I'm a happy person here." She changed her first name, and she's happier.

Yulahlia recently graduated from law school, and she is a lawyer for disabled children and adults who are entitled to special services. She told me recently, "I never thought I would say this, but the rape made me rethink who I am. I was into partying and drinking then. And he made me feel like nothing. Now I think, why should some man make *me* feel that way. I'm a great person, really. And now I know it." When she told me she still "checks in" with her feelings at work and in her personal life, I decided to call the places you could connect with in this book Check Ins.

Even if something very bad happens to you, you can use it to become who you want to be. You can take control of your life, just like my niece did.

Of course, some girls have experiences that are very different from Anna's, Ellen's, Anita's, and mine. Two sisters who came to Girls Speak Out in New York City spoke freely in the workshops both days about subjects that are usually taboo. Their parents wanted to meet me when I asked the girls to come back to more workshops and to give me advice, so I arranged a visit to their family's apartment in Harlem.

Susan and Allan, the girls' parents, grew up in the same two-block area where they now live with their daughters, ten-year-old Tina and thirteen-year-old Stephanie. I visited on a Saturday in July when Allan and Susan were home from work, and Susan's sister stopped by with her two-year-old grandson.

Tina was at the kitchen table with us, painting with watercolors, decorating a picture of a hot air balloon, and she listened attentively as her mother talked about "telling children the truth." Susan said she told both girls about problems like sexual abuse when they were ten years old. Tina said she felt better knowing what could happen, and she said her mother told her that if someone bothered her, even if it was her mother or her father, another relative or a friend, Tina should tell someone.

"It makes me feel safe," Tina told me. "I like knowing what to do."

Allan brought us cold drinks, then he sat down and leaned forward in his seat, with his chin in his hands.

"I'm proud of my daughters," he said. "We wish they could travel and see more of this country, and maybe they will do more than we have. I hope so."

Telling

How do Ellen's and Yulahlia's stories make *you* feel? People who study young girls say that another characteristic of nine- and ten-year-old girls, besides the optimism and self-confidence I mentioned before, is that they say what they feel out loud even if everyone else is reluctant to say it. Remember, it's never too late to talk to someone you trust about something that hurts you.

Have you had any hurtful experiences you want to tell someone? Writing or drawing is a way of telling what's happening to you, too, if speaking words aloud is hard, but you'll know when you're ready, just as other girls have known.

You may want to write about your ideas on how to be a good friend and protector, especially of yourself. Linda, a twelve-year-old girl in San Diego, told us she had a friend who was an incest victim—which means that someone in her own family was abusing her. Her friend kept it a secret until she told Linda. Now Linda is encouraging her to tell a grown-up she trusts. In the meantime, Linda says, she's careful to protect her friend's privacy and safety, and her own feelings. The best thing that happened, Linda's friend told her, is that instead of blaming herself for her father's abuse, she says, "I know it's not my fault." Why do you think this makes her feel better?

Stephanie was preparing her high school applications, and when she came into the kitchen, we talked about her choices.

"Something good will happen, sooner or later. That's what I believe, you know," Stephanie told me as I left.

"Don't let Harlem's negative reputation, which isn't true in this neighborhood, keep you from walking downtown on a nice day like this. You'll be okay," Allan told me.

As I walked to my friend Gloria's house, I was thinking about how hopeful this family is about life. I couldn't wait to talk about how good it is to be with a family who talks openly about their feelings across the kitchen table—and to someday share this experience with you, too.

Bad things can happen to girls, and things such as sexual and physical abuse do happen more often to girls than to boys, but girls around the world have shown that they can heal and even grow stronger after being hurt or abused. I'm grateful that the workshops and this book are places where we can learn about negative things that can affect girls, but we also learn about girls' strength and their incredible ability to overcome obstacles.

CHANGING WHAT'S UNFAIR

Always speak your mind
and that's when
you're powerful.
—Shakoiya

On a second workshop day, one fourteen-year-old girl said, "We've had times that were sacred in the first workshop, and afterward you feel so close." Now that we've finished reading *Finding the Green Stone*, it's time to think and talk about when we can be our true selves. As you read this chapter, think about the challenges that girls and women face, and what changes would improve females' lives.

In a workshop in South Carolina, one of the women, thirty-three-year-old Roberta, was the first to speak. She told us that two important things had happened to her during the week since our first meeting, and they both involved her green stone. First, she had held her green stone in her hand when she asked for a raise at work; she manages a store and when she was promoted to manager, she didn't get a raise. She got one this time because, she said, "I felt like it was fair and asking was what I needed to do." The green stone had given her the courage to ask for what she thought she deserved.

Roberta then told us that she is going to divorce her husband. She said "he can't be a good father" to her two daughters, ages two and twelve. She said the green stone is a reminder to her that she could have a better life.

One of the last girls to talk that morning was Jasmine, a twelve-year-old girl. She started by telling us that her week had started out awful. Her brother, who's seventeen, is a drug addict. He had been living away from home, but Jasmine told us that he had come back and stolen "everything that's precious to us." He even took her collection of glass animals. Jasmine said he's in jail now and she felt sad about that.

Roberta spoke again: "Jasmine, I'm sorry about your brother. I want you to know you're braver than I was. When I talked about my husband, about how I was leaving him, I didn't tell the whole truth, the real reason I'm leaving. My husband is a drug addict, just like your brother. When you were talking about your brother, I realized I had been ashamed to talk about my husband. I thought it was my job to make him stop using drugs. He's making our lives miserable.

"But I think I can do something to help my daughters—and myself. I want to thank you. I want you to know you're not alone. There are a lot of us who will change things."

Jasmine also told us that even though she is sad about her brother, she is angry with him, too. Having these different feelings at once, she said, is "okay, not a problem." Jasmine had also written in her journal for the first time during the week; maybe, she said, she'd write a story about her brother. Writing things down privately does help us to understand them.

In other cities, girls have said different things. Jen, who's ten and lives in northern California, told us she "felt physically and emotionally stronger all week." In New York City, six girls all between the ages of fifteen and eighteen discovered they "didn't have time" to be their true selves. They were involved in so many activities, including long phone conversations helping other girls and boys with problems and leaving them no time to concentrate on themselves. Sharon, a seventeen-year-old, said, "I feel pressure to take advantage of every opportunity to add another activity to my college application."

One sixteen-year-old girl took me aside and said, "This may sound weird, Andrea, but my green stone made me feel better all week." I told her I thought she was feeling good about herself, and she agreed, "That's it. That's what it is."

One ten-year-old in West Virginia brought more than her green stone to the second workshop. Meghan brought a small wooden box full of what she described as "all the things that are most important to me in the world." She opened the lid, and inside the box was a collection of objects, each with a story.

"Here's my favorite book, *A Wrinkle in Time*, that's about finding good no matter where you travel in the universe. This is a kachina doll I made in school in third grade, and this is a dream catcher I bought at a street fair last year."

Meghan took out a blue plastic calculator that was missing the display screen. Although the calculator was broken, it was clean and new looking.

"I don't know why I keep this," Meghan said. "I found it in the park, took it home, cleaned it up, and put it in my box. I've had it for about a year now."

The girl sitting next to Meghan said, "Maybe you keep it to remind you that you have power inside you, not in a machine, and you don't need a machine to be powerful."

Meghan said she was worried she wasn't being her true self. But that morning, she and her dad listened to music together.

"My dad loves music," she said, "and so do I. When we were listening to Bach together, well, I love it so much, it felt so good; I knew it then.

"My true self is music. Music makes me feel all kinds of things. About love, and how my dad loves baseball, especially one player, Keith Hernandez. Keith Hernandez plays baseball because he loves it. Most of the other players do it for money. I've been thinking a lot about money.

"I think greed is the reason for a lot of problems. I think it happens all over the world. And not just to people; we get greedy about nature and animals, too. When we forget about our true selves, we get greedy."

Taking Charge at School

Fourteen-year-old Yvonne, who goes to a middle school in Harlem, returned to the second workshop with a story about school. She asked right away if she could lead the reading, and she seemed excited. Her friends from school who were there also teased her when she started to read out loud, but she ignored them and went right on reading. Then she told her story about being her true self.

During the week, in Yvonne's English class, they had been discussing a book, *That Was Then, This Is Now*. Yvonne said that the boys in the class had been making it impossible to talk. The book is about two boys who are friends, and Yvonne's male classmates had been calling the characters "homos" and "fags." They had disrupted what anyone else said, especially Yvonne, because she wasn't afraid to disagree with them.

The teacher had asked the boys to be quiet. Yvonne had told them to be quiet. She had said she wanted to talk about the book without their noise. They hadn't stopped. Yvonne had gotten up from her seat, said she'd be right back, and left the classroom.

"I marched down the hall, around the corner, and into the principal's office. I told her that it was her job to make sure I could learn. I said the boys were making it impossible for me to learn anything. They were making rude remarks about the book, and I didn't appreciate them or their sexist remarks."

While she was telling us what she had done, Yvonne kept on looking down and tying and retying her shoelaces. The girls from her school who had teased her earlier, when she was reading, were now quiet. She continued.

"Well, the principal got up and told me to come with her back to my class. She went into the room with me, and the boys were still laughing. The principal told the boys that they would have detention, and everyone would stay in at lunch to talk about what happened during class.

"What I don't understand," Yvonne said, "is that later on in the day, some of the boys thanked me."

When I heard Yvonne say this about the boys in her class, I thought that they were like Johnny in *Finding the Green Stone*, and I thought that she was like Katie, even though she didn't think of it that way. The boys were grateful because Yvonne was giving them the chance to be free of the pressure to be thoughtless. They really wanted to be friends with girls, but they found it hard to do that in their school.

Yvonne's friend Maria interrupted to say, "Some of the boys told us they didn't like what the others were saying, but they thought it was better to go along with the program."

Yvonne said, "Well, I'm glad it was me who got up and complained. I know I'm going to make it, that being a girl is tough in class, but I'm getting good grades and I know where I'm going. I've made up my mind."

Her friends were now encouraging Yvonne to continue her story.

"The principal said that she was going to change the punishment system. She said students should be rewarded when they do good things, and not just punished for getting into trouble. She called my mom, and my mom called my aunts, and now my whole family knows. Now everyone's talking about what I did, like it was some big deal." Yvonne was smiling down at her boots as she finished talking.

In Arizona, during the first workshop, a sixth-grader talked about drugs on her school campus. Doreen said some of her friends were smoking pot during recess, and they offered her some. "I feel afraid when they offer it to me," she said. "And I didn't know what to do."

Doreen decided to tell the principal. She talked it over with her mother and decided she wanted to do it herself. Her mother said she should tell the principal to call her at home if he wanted to talk to her, too. One of her friends who kept offering her drugs didn't have a supportive family, and Doreen said smoking pot made her friend feel accepted at school. It's a small school in a rural area, and Doreen was worried about what might happen to the kids. She was very nervous but determined to make it safer at school.

"The principal really didn't do anything," Doreen told us with a shrug of her shoulder. "He said it was hard to catch kids in the act, and he didn't want to do anything illegal. I think I knew nothing much was going to happen, but I had to do it anyway. My mom says she's going to get on the school board. If there was someone else who felt the same way I do, and I hope to find at least one other student, I think I'd do a petition or something. It would make me feel better, I guess."

Handling Peer Pressure in School

Doreen and Yvonne are the first among their friends to speak out about something that's unfair. At first, Yvonne's friends seemed to be having trouble with her leadership, and they teased her in front of the whole class. Why do you think her friends were uncomfortable? What pressure do you feel from friends to "go along with the program" rather than speak out? What change in her friends and in herself has taken place by the time Yvonne finishes telling her story? Do you have any suggestions about how Yvonne's and Doreen's friends might have acted toward her that would have been supportive despite the risks? Doreen acted without her friends. How do you feel about her mother's involvement? (I've discovered that if an adult speaks out in support of a girl, it is usually her mother.) Petitions can be a very effective means of change, but asking people to sign them can be risky, especially if your friends seem uncomfortable about taking a stand. When, if ever, is it important to risk a friendship to do what you feel is the right thing to do?

How often do you feel peer pressure at school? Make a list of what you would change in a class or at your school. You may want to consider what being accepted at school means to you.

Changing the Rules

Sometimes knowing exactly what will help to change things is challenging, especially if you're in a new place with a new set of rules, and you don't know if anyone will support you. Each town, neighborhood, and family has a list of supposed-to rules for females. Author and teacher Esmeralda Santiago writes in her book *When I Was Puerto Rican* about how these rules affect a teenager who moved from a small town in Puerto Rico to New York City. The girl's first lessons about school in Puerto Rico are like those in most countries; they're filled with supposed-tos.

> *I started school in the middle of the hurricane season, and the world grew suddenly bigger, a vast place of other adults and children whose lives were similar, but whose shadings I couldn't really explore out of respect and* dignidad. Dignidad *was something you conferred on other people, and they, in turn, gave it back to you. It meant you never swore at people, never showed anger in front of strangers, never stared, never stood too close to people you'd just met. . . . It meant adults had to be referred to as Don so-and-so, and Doña so-and-so, except for teachers who you should call Mister or Missis so-and-so. It meant if you were a child, you did not speak until spoken to, did not look an adult in the eye, did not raise your voice nor enter or leave a room without permission. It meant adults were always right, especially if they were old. It meant men could look at women any way they liked, but women could never look at men directly, only in sidelong glances. . . . It meant you didn't gossip, tattle, or tease. It meant men could say things to women as they walked down the street, but women couldn't say anything to men, not even to tell them to go jump in the harbor and leave them alone.*
>
> *All these rules entered our household the minute I was allowed to leave for the long walk to and from school. It wasn't that I hadn't learned them before . . .*
>
> *But these rules had little to do with the way we lived at home. In our family we fought with vigor, adults as well as children, even though we knew we weren't supposed to. We yelled across the room at one another, came in and out of our one-room house*

without saying "excuse me" and "may I come in," or even knocking. . . . We children spoke whenever we felt like it, interrupted our parents all the time, and argued with them until Mami finally reminded us that we had stepped over the line of what was considered respectful behavior towards parents.

Different Places, Different Practices

Lily is a nineteen-year-old Puerto Rican woman going to college in California who came to our workshops. When she was growing up, she had been told not to touch valuable things that didn't belong to her. In the first workshop, she noticed that Latina girls were reluctant to pick up and handle the ancient artifacts. When Lily explained to the girls that the rules were different in Girls Speak Out, they relaxed and examined each artifact.

Differences in ideas about how to behave can be cultural; that is, these ideas come from rules we learn from parents, relatives, and seeing what people around us do. I think of cultural differences as behaviors and ideas we learn from the outside in, but it's important to understand them so you don't misinterpret what other people do. (For instance, in some African traditions, it's a sign of respect for young people to look down at the floor when talking to elders, but in this country people equate honesty with "looking you in the eye.")

Even people in the same culture may share none, some, or all of the same rules. In Girls Speak Out, knowing about cultural influences has brought us closer together; it would've been easy to think the Latina girls didn't like the artifacts, but once Lily spoke up, we all had a great time holding and passing them around. It felt like a party.

There are also some cultural practices that do permanent physical damage to females. A woman who came here from Africa didn't want her young daughters to be victims of *female genital mutilation* (FGM). In much of Africa and some parts of the USA and Europe, defenders of FGM surgically remove part or all of a young girl's outer genitals, especially the clitoris, so she won't be able to feel sexual pleasure and be tempted to "misbehave." Girls' vaginas are often sewn closed so they can't have intercourse until they're married. It's a very painful practice, and also damaging to a girl's health.

The African girls' mother stayed in the USA in order to protect her daughters from undergoing FGM in their native country. The girls didn't come to Girls Speak Out because they still didn't feel safe, but they did read this book, which was safe.

Mimi, an Ethiopian woman who's living in California, explained that some Africans living in the USA practice female genital mutilation. Mimi had been a victim of FGM in her own country when she was six years old, and she had recently asked her mother why she had let it happen to Mimi. Her mother told Mimi that she was following tradition, that she and her mother, Mimi's grandmother, were also victims. Her mother said she was sorry it had happened to Mimi. She then traveled with Mimi to villages in Ethiopia and urged women not to allow their daughters to be mutilated. This is not easy because a girl whose parents believe in FGM may not be considered marriageable without it.

As you see, in Girls Speak Out we learn important things about other cultures from girls and women from those cultures. Mary, a young woman in Oregon, has a Japanese-American boyfriend, and she brought his two teenage sisters to the first workshop of the program. During the week between workshops, they told her they were uncomfortable because girls and women in Girls Speak Out had talked about sex, sexual abuse, and neglect. The Japanese-American girls had been taught not to talk in

Reacting to Sexism

Reading about practices like FGM and incest can make us feel scared, angry, confused, and sad almost at the same time. Sometimes we react so angrily that we want to do something physical to release our feelings. It's okay, for instance, to tear a piece of paper into pieces and beat a punching bag if it releases your anger. If we keep feelings like rage and sadness inside, they will keep trying to surface or explode even during adulthood. How do you express anger or the sorrow it hides? What would you like to do that you haven't done? Mimi, a victim of FGM, said, "My anger was really a deep sadness that I was afraid would drown me. I learned it was better to talk about my anger and admit how sad I was or I would always carry it with me." What is your reaction to her philosophy?

Your notebook is one place to express your emotions. Without using words, create an impression of your reactions to FGM and other unfair practices that can damage your body, your spirit, or your self-confidence, and make you feel unhappy, frightened, or insecure. Create a mural, which uses many pictures on one page to tell a story, or make a collage using torn and crumpled paper, fabric, or natural materials such as leaves, pebbles, and twigs. You can use sounds, too, to express your reactions by composing music, drumming, or playing another instrument. Once we safely release sadness and anger, we create more room in our lives for joy and laughter.

public about "personal matters." Because they had also been taught not to bring attention to themselves, they didn't talk to us about their feelings during the workshop.

When Mary told me the sisters didn't want to come back to the second workshop, we worked out an arrangement: Mary would leave with them if they were uncomfortable.

Milly, a writer who helped me develop Girls Speak Out, is Chinese-American. Milly was at a workshop with girls who talked about being victims of sexual abuse. Months after the workshop, Milly told me she had felt "frozen" with these girls. She had never been around girls who talked so openly about such difficult experiences, and it was hard for her to feel okay about them. She wasn't neglected or abused during her childhood. She felt it was awful for girls to be treated so badly, and she was trying to overcome the cultural behavior she had learned as a girl that forbid talking about sexual abuse. Milly wants to be more open with people whose experiences are different from hers, especially when discussing difficult topics that can help someone.

The next excerpt from *When I Was Puerto Rican* is about learning something positive from a painful experience. One of the sexist rules in Esmeralda's culture is that women stay at home, but her mother works outside the house in a factory. Esmeralda is disappointed to learn how the neighbors feel about her mother's choice.

> *I got the message that my mother was breaking a taboo that I'd never heard about. The women in the neighborhood turned their backs on her when they saw her coming, or, when they talked to her, they scanned the horizon, as if looking at her would infect them with whatever had made her go out and get a job.*

Esmeralda isn't happy either when her mother tells her what she's doing:

"Where are you going?"

"There's a new factory opening in Toa Baja. Maybe they need people who can sew."

"Who's going to take care of us?"

"Gloria will be here in a little while. You can help her with the kids. I've already made dinner."

"Will you work every day?"

"If they hire me."

"So you won't be around all the time."

"We need the money. . . ."

Mami twisted and sprayed her hair, powdered her face, patted rouge on already pink cheeks, and spread lipstick over already red lips. . . . I wanted to find a rag and wipe that stuff off her face, the way she wiped off the dirt and grime that collected on mine. She turned to me with a large red smile.

"What do you think?"

I was ashamed to look, afraid to speak what I saw.

"Well?"

. . . I couldn't help the tears that broke my face into a million bits, which made her kneel and hold me. I wrapped my arms around her, but what I felt was not Mami but the harsh bones of her undergarments. I buried my face in the soft space between her neck and shoulder, and sought there the fragrance of oregano and rosemary, but all I could come up with was Cashmere Bouquet and the faint flowery dust of Maybelline.

At the end of the book, Esmeralda is about to begin high school. She and her mother are now living in New York City. One day she tells her mother . . .

"I hate my life!" I yelled.

"Then do something about it," she yelled back.

Esmeralda follows her mother's advice and example. She auditions for a special high school in New York City that encourages students to act, write, and be artists and musicians. Her life changes when she discovers that being creative, especially as a writer, makes her happy. She leaves her anger behind and makes a positive future for herself.

Remember when I mentioned the fact that stories about female human beings are missing from history books? In Girls Speak Out, we have personal books with girls' *and* women's histories that are created in workshops and in notebooks like the one you use for Check Ins. In workshops, girls' writings and drawings are distributed to workshop participants in the booklets I already mentioned that are a miniature version of this book. There's also a list in the booklets of good books that have been published for girls. You'll find your own book list at the back of this book.

It's exciting to have history books about us, especially ones that we've written ourselves. Your notebook is your personal history book, and it may be private and not for other people's eyes, but if you're like me, there are probably some writings and/or drawings you'd like to share with other people. Some girls hand out copies to their closest friends. Some girls have shown their creations to a lot of people. You can send your creations to me to read or I can post them on my website if you want many people to see them. What you create in your notebook, or in some other way, can stay private or be shared with the public. It's another choice you may make for yourself. Girls Speak Out is a place where girls can find each other in a variety of ways.

Organizing a Talk Show

My true self
is being generous.
—Melissa

Now it's time for a Girls Speak Out talk show. Girls originated the talk show idea at the very beginning of the Girls Speak Out workshops. It has been the chosen activity in every second workshop except one. In that workshop, girls talked for hours without using the talk show format. They asked each other and the women question after question. We stayed an extra hour until finally we had to leave the room.

As I mentioned earlier, girls and their bodies is the most popular talk show topic. Participants in workshops haven't discussed more than one topic in a talk show because time flies. Other topics that have been voted on include "Children Having Children," "The Way People Portray Females in Today's World," and "Should Teachers Put Their Hands on Other People's Children?" These talk shows are usually live and unrehearsed because we have a limited amount of time.

You can decide how much time to spend on a talk show because you're going to plan it in a special way. You can take as much time as you need, and you can use the following information from other Girls Speak Out talk shows to guide you as you imagine or organize your own show. You can build on what girls have done before you.

Most of the time, in workshop talk shows, girls fifteen years old and younger create and run the talk show while older workshop members watch, help when they are requested to, and ask questions during the show. Everyone helps with transforming the room into a talk show studio. You will probably need help, too. Make sure you have a big newsprint pad and markers to use for taking notes and making signs. Folding chairs are arranged in rows or in a semicircle facing the stage for the audience to sit in. Four or five chairs for guests are placed onstage, and these face the audience. We keep it simple because we have a short amount of time in a workshop, but you can use more comfortable chairs and place decorations like plants and use pictures from your collection onstage.

Girls decide who's going to have which job in the talk show. We have a host who asks questions, an announcer who introduces people, and guests who appear onstage to talk about the topic. Other girls can be technicians who manage props such as microphones and water pitchers; producers who prepare the guests; or backstage and audience helpers. You can hold auditions and ask friends to vote or you can choose your favorite cast.

When it's time for girls to rehearse, older girls and women leave the studio to help prepare lunch since we eat as soon as the show ends. Pizza is a favorite lunch and snack food in the USA and Canada, as long as there are veggie pizzas as well as meat pizzas, because there's always at least one girl who's a vegetarian. Do you have a favorite snack or lunch food? Perhaps your parents or siblings can help prepare food for you and the cast and crew.

Planning Your Talk Show

Here is a list of details that you can use in planning your talk show:

- Girls wrap a marker in construction paper, transforming it into a microphone. During the show, it's passed back and forth from speaker to speaker.
- A sign on an easel announces the name of the talk show and the topic. Sometimes the talk show is named for a girl, usually the hostess, or you can use the name of a city, town, TV station, or website—or you can make up a name.
- Any commercials for your talk show need to be planned ahead, but what usually happens in the workshop is that the girls are so busy organizing the show itself that there's no time to prepare commercials. Workshops have stayed commercial free, but you are creating a tradition for your own Girls Speak Out talk show, and maybe you think commercials would be fun.
- Girls who will be onstage stay out of sight until the host comes out to introduce the show.
- Our talk show guests are usually friends who have different opinions about how to dress, when to date, and whether to have sex; sometimes girls pretend to be mothers and celebrities.

Talk Show Surprises

Sometimes things don't happen as expected, and most of the time what happens spontaneously is fun. Guest experts usually forget to talk about the book they're holding as a prop. Instead, they talk about their own experiences and feelings, and the audience usually loves it.

Experts have said the following that made us smile:

- "I have a diagnosis. It's a state of being mixed-up."
- "We're on TV, and we want to look like we recycle our water cups so don't look for the wastebasket."
- When a hostess asked an expert to give her opinion to a mother and daughter who repeatedly disagreed about what age the daughter had to be to date, the expert shook her head no and said, "They're already up to the limit of being influenced. We all need a break."

A talk show topic can be explosive. During workshop talk shows, disagreements have been strong about whether a girl can do what she wants and not care about what other people think of her, especially when it comes to how she dresses. Two girls in Chicago argued about whether a girl's choice of clothing affects her friends as well as herself. "I don't want to be with you when you wear sexy stuff," one girl said to her talk show friend. "You look like you want boys all over you."

Her friend said the way she dressed was her business, and she didn't care what boys thought.

"You look like you're asking for it," her friend argued.

"I'm not, and I can dress any way I want to."

Clothes Talk

Do you have any strong feelings about what you or other girls wear? Do you stereotype girls depending on their clothing? How do you feel when boys stereotype girls' fashions? What suggestions, if any, do you have about clothing that girls should avoid wearing or be free to wear? Write a dialogue between a mother and a daughter or between two friends who disagree about fashionable or religious clothing. For instance, a school outfit that reveals a girl's body in a way that may be fashionable, such as low-slung jeans or see-through tops, may outrage one character. Wearing scarves across your face as a religious custom or wearing a burka that wraps a body from head to toe, leaving only the eyes visible, could be the trigger for a dialogue, too.

How safe do you feel when you leave your house? Are some places such as school safer than others to wear certain styles? What would you wear if you could wear anything you wanted to? Design a dream outfit for yourself. Imagine where you would wear it.

The talk show host said, "I think we can go outside in a flannel nightgown, wearing a bag over our heads, and guys would still give us trouble."

Audience Participation Time

Often the audience, the host, and the onstage experts have a conversation during the talk show. Here are a few of the most popular audience-participation discussions. In Toronto, Canada, talk show members and the audience exchanged personal stories about whether it was ever "too late" or whether you could be "too old" to do something, like go to school and start a new career. The girls led the discussion from the stage, and someone ran through the audience with the microphone (which started to disintegrate from so much handling).

One woman participant, Cindy, said she had been to a woman's conference in China, and she had discovered that Chinese orphans had very hard lives. She decided to adopt a Chinese baby girl. She and her husband are fifty-four, and their other children are grown up. Cindy said, "You're never too old."

Nine-year-old Becky said she loved playing soccer at school, but the boys always complained about having a girl on their team. She was also tired of being the last person picked to play and of the faces the boys made when her name was finally called. Becky's friends told her she'd never change the boys' attitude.

When they had to choose players the past week, Becky said she had told the boys how she felt about their attitude. She had stood in the middle of the group and asked them how they would feel if they were treated like they had no feelings. "I know you care about winning, and I can help you win," she had told them, "but you have to be fair." She said she felt better. The boys had listened, and Becky said she'd do it again and again "if I have to."

Ruth has just started school, and she's studying to become a teacher. Ruth married just after she graduated from high school, and her husband died recently. She's forty-four, and said she "never imagined" she'd be able to support herself and her family.

I talked about graduating from law school when I was forty. I had always wanted to be a lawyer, but when I was young, I was told that girls didn't grow up to be lawyers. Well, it turned out that I didn't either, but I still wanted to learn about law and how the legal system works. Law school gave me the confidence to try new things, like becoming an investigative reporter and building a house on a mountaintop.

Talking about Sexual Harassment

Girls in New York City, like girls everywhere whom I've visited, wanted to talk about sexual harassment, especially in school. Although they don't like it, girls agree that sexual harassment is part of what happens when a girl's body changes. *Sexual harassment* means words or actions—by anyone, not only by teachers or someone who has power over you—that focus on your body, make you feel uncomfortable, and keep you from working well in school or on the job.

The girls had a problem with a principal at their school, who was "always putting his hands on our backs, heads, and our shoulders. He's always rubbing us and laughing about it." In South Carolina, a teacher and some other students referred to how girls' bodies looked in ways that made girls feel uncomfortable.

The teacher said things like, "You're too pretty to worry about that" and "You look good in short skirts."

"It's like you're a thing, not a person," said Loretta. Boys in gym class teased the girls about wearing bras and developing breasts. Running and playing sports that made a girl's breasts bounce brought on a lot of the boys' comments and made the girls not want to run. Most of the adults to whom the girls complained didn't think it was so bad. They said things like, "Boys will be boys" and "What did you expect now that you're becoming a woman?"

When I was teaching in a middle school (sixth to eighth grade), I was also writing for a newspaper in northern California. I knew four girls who had been sexually harassed by their high school drama teacher, and I helped them confront the school. My son, Jesse, had gone to the same high school as the girls. When I started helping them, I asked Jesse if he had known what was happening between the girls and their teacher. He told me everyone had known something was going on, but no one had ever really talked about it. When one of the girls let Jesse read her description of what had happened, I remember the look on his face as he handed it back to me. I think it changed him because he said, "I had no idea what it felt like to be her in that situation. I wish it hadn't happened, and that I had understood what it felt like. I was senior class president, and maybe I could have done something to help." When I told her what Jesse had said, she didn't feel so alone.

We discovered that teachers, principals, and other people working in schools don't know it's against the law for girls to be sexually harassed by adults or other students. They think that sexual harassment laws are only for grown-ups in the workplace. People outside the school system should learn about girls' rights, too. No matter what, as girls and women work together, we can become experts on topics, such as sexual harassment, that are important to us.

Sometimes girls ask me to be a guest on their talk show, and I tell what has happened to girls in the USA. It surprises me how many girls around the world, in big cities, villages, and small towns, have had similar experiences. One of these girls is named Nihura, and she lives in Namibia, Africa. Like the girls in the USA, she had to find a way to protect and assert herself.

Nihura wrote to me after she read this book because she wanted to discuss how to help improve the lives of Namibian females. While she was in high school, she organized a Girls Speak Out club with female and male members who found ways to make things better for females. They exchanged personal experiences, marched in local parades in support of females' rights, and wrote letters about unfair practices to local newspapers. Last year, when

Nihura went to college, she worked in an office in her school, and her boss sexually harassed her: "He would touch me and make remarks that made me feel uncomfortable and afraid." The other women in the office told her to ignore the behavior, but Nihura deeply believes in girls' and women's rights, and she couldn't pretend sexual harassment was normal.

When Nihura asked me for advice, I suggested we find a woman in Namibia who works for women's rights because I wanted someone near her to help Nihura to feel strong *and* safe. An organization in New York City called Equality Now has a network of women around the world just as Girls Speak Out has a network of girls in different countries. Equality Now helped us find a woman who agreed to support Nihura. She said, "I felt better just having people listen to me, especially people who know about girls' rights in my country. I told the woman in my office that his behavior was wrong. When my boss left the office, I was relieved and I felt empowered." Nihura is planning on attending law school to be a girls' and women's rights activist.

The USA has a law that protects children in school called Title IX of the Civil Rights Act. Title IX says that girls and boys are guaranteed an equal education, free from harassment and discrimination. Harassing or restricting you based on your gender, race, sexual preference, ability, or religion is illegal. Each school is supposed to inform students and their families about their rights under Title IX. Knowing about the law helped four girls I was working with, but it still took a long time for the teacher to lose his California teaching credential, and then he went to another state to teach. Sometimes it takes years, decades, or even centuries before change occurs, but every effort to resist what's unfair helps make change happen.

One of the students I worked with in California is named Willow. Willow realized she could do something about being sexually harassed in 1992, when she heard Anita Hill on television. Anita Hill was a witness against Clarence Thomas, who wanted a lifetime job as a judge on the United States Supreme Court. Anita said Clarence Thomas had sexually harassed her years before, when he was her boss.

Willow said she learned from Anita Hill's testimony that it was against the law for someone in authority to treat people unfairly because of their sex, and she complained to her school about her teacher. Some girls in Girls Speak Out are worried that they could "get into trouble for telling on a teacher." They wonder whether you might "get a bad grade?" Some adults worry, as I did, about Nihura taking a stand in a place where it may be dangerous for girls to speak out and there may be fewer adults who will support her, but girls and women are successfully protecting each other even when they live on different continents.

Willow said telling was "scary. I stopped going to drama practice after school, and then I dropped the drama class." But, she said, "It was worse when he was harassing me and other girls. I hated having him touching me and talking to me about his wife and having sex.

"I'm glad I complained. A lot of other girls told me they had the same problem with him. Some of the other girls were angry because they thought he was a good teacher, but I didn't want him to do it to other girls. It took a long time to make him stop, but it was worth it. I couldn't have done it alone. I'm glad there were other girls and women in our community, and I had my mother to help out.

"If I could say something to girls, I'd tell them to believe in themselves. I think most of us know when something is wrong, but we don't listen to our instincts."

It was hard for Anita Hill to talk about what happened to her, especially on television. She took her mother and father with her

Stopping Sexual Harassment

Anita Hill said, "Now that I've found my voice, I'm never going to be silent." When Anita wrote a book about her experiences, she entitled it, *Speaking Truth to Power*. Do you think you would feel the same as Anita, Nihura, and Willow? What suggestions do you have about stopping sexual harassment?

One girl who was a talk show expert told us she started a campaign in her school to stop peer sexual harassment, which is usually boys teasing girls, especially at recess, in the hallways, and on the way to and from school. She placed a complaint box in the school office, and students on her committee reviewed the complaints. Students and teachers met, and they learned how to stop the harassment. What ideas do you have about ways to protect girls from being sexually harassed by students and/or teachers?

to Washington, D.C., when she went to talk about Clarence Thomas to the United States Senate committee that was deciding whether he could be a Supreme Court justice.

One of Anita's sisters is a fourth-grade teacher in Oklahoma. She went into her principal's office to see Anita on television when Anita was testifying. The men from the Senate who were questioning Anita obviously didn't believe her. Her sister could see how hard it was for Anita, so she arranged to leave school that day, and she went to Washington, D.C., to support her. When she returned, her class was glad she had gone even though they had missed her. Anita's whole family went to support her when she spoke out.

Even if a law like Title IX isn't passed or followed in your country, you can feel powerful if you understand that girls have rights. "Pretending" to be an expert can lead to actually becoming an expert. That's just one of the many examples of what you can learn from putting together your own talk show, and talking about what's happening to you and your friends.

I hope reading about these talk shows helps you explore where, when, and how you can find ways to express your voice in the company of other girls who can make a difference and change what's unfair.

As True Selves Grow Up

The things that I think make me a young woman are my heart, mind, and body.

—Andy

By now, we're almost at the end of the workshops and this book. After the talk show, sitting in a circle brings us together again, girls and women, side by side. Perhaps you can arrange your picture collection, artifact, notebook, and other special objects around you as you read.

This chapter is different because you'll be reading a mixture of selections about what it means to be young, to become a woman, and to grow old. One of the reasons women are part of the workshops is because I've discovered that many girls are convinced that they must give up their true selves in order to grow up, and meeting women who are still their true selves is inspiring. Happily, a true self lasts a lifetime.

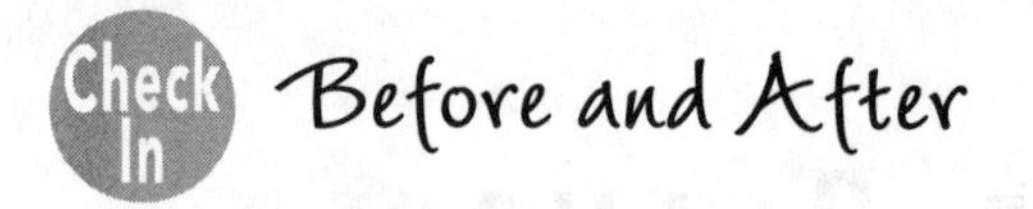

Answer these questions now and again after you have finished reading this chapter. Who or what has the greatest influence on you? What do you need to be a strong and happy woman? Do you have what you need? How will you get it?

Feelings Here, There, and Everywhere

In *Little Jordan*, Marly Youmans's first novel, thirteen-year-old Meg has a special summer where . . .

> *. . . my weeks at the beach blended into one week, one day . . . I learned about distance and about seeing at close range that summer. I believed what I touched with my hands. That summer I was busy running up against things, learning what they meant.*

Meg begins to look at boys differently, and they see her differently, especially Fred Massey, who . . .

> *. . . was fifteen, (and) good looking. . . . He had the sort of intent expression on his face that makes people say that somebody's eyebrows are drawn together. Honestly, my stomach dropped an inch or two when I met his blue eyes. Not that I stood alone in that kind of behavior. Half the girls in our school had crushes on Fred Massey.*

Meg and Fred share time and secrets over the next few weeks.

> *"You're a strange girl, Meg," Fred said. He sighed, as if he'd been holding his breath.*
>
> *Neither of us said a word for a long time.*

"I guess I'll go home some day soon," he said, sitting up.

"Because I'm strange?" I felt sure I would cry, partly because Fred was going home. . . .

"No." Fred laughed then, and he put his arm around my shoulders—touching me for the first time. He gazed up at the hill fields. . . .

"Yesterday," he said, still looking up at the hills, "my mom told me that running away from one thing just leads you to chase after another."

That gave me a quirk of surprise, and I was busy puzzling over what it meant when Fred leaned closer and rubbed his face against mine. Then he kissed me . . . very quietly. Quiet as dew. For a minute I saw his eyelashes against his skin and felt his cheek, cool and smooth like a little boy's cheek.

Maybe all first kisses are the same, or maybe none of them are. Mine started with thinking about a boy's mother, a boy's cheek. Then suddenly everything seemed to change, as though I had stepped into deep water, and I closed my eyes.

Different Loving Relationships

Have you imagined what your first romantic kiss would be like? Have you experienced it already? How did it compare to what you imagined? Meg says her first kiss changed her. How do you feel about a romantic relationship? Do you believe it could be powerful enough to change you? Which relationships are most important to you? Where is romance on your list of relationships?

In a different way, Meg's feelings for her grandmother are as strong and deep as they are for her boyfriend, especially as Meg discovers more about who her grandmother was and is.

My grandma met me on the bleached, silvery porch, and I loved her more than ever, even though earlier I had thought maybe I was getting so grown-up that a grandmother might not mean as much. Because in between visits you forget how she smells of lilacs and how soft her skin is, you forget how an old person is really just as interesting as anybody else, maybe more so if we're talking about my grandparents.

Meg spends an afternoon with her grandmother on the water, exploring tidal creeks in her grandmother's canoe. Meg is asking her grandmother about her hair, which is coiled in a neat wheel at the nape of her neck.

"When you let down your hair—" I hesitated.

Grandma thrust the canoe off a snag.

"How long is it?" I asked.

"Why did you think of that? I don't know. Long. Not so long as it used to be. Old people droop and change. Noses get bigger, ears and feet, too. Hair, hair thins and breaks."

"You must have had an awful lot of hair when you were young," I said.

"Yes, I did. Everyone said thick hair was a woman's great beauty, but I hardly knew what to do with it all."

I had a sudden vivid picture of Grandma like Eve in an oil painting, a young and pretty Eve with scads of silvery hair. Only of course it wouldn't be silver. It would be a color like mine. It would sweep over her bare shoulders, splashing past her feet. My grandpa, with his young man's hands, would be weaving his fingers through her hair, unplaiting and combing out her braids.

Somewhere beyond the frame where they played as lovers and Grandpa combed my grandma's hair, Momma would be snoozing, a baby, her mouth open like a bird's. I lay there too, half of me, an infinitely small egg sleeping in my child-Momma's body.

Now here was my grandma, talking to me as though I was a grown woman.

"At night he combed my hair until it untangled and the brush sank through easily, as through water. He said that to lie in bed with my hair was like sleeping on the waves. . . ."

"That was a sweet time in my life."

Grandma laid the paddle across the canoe. She leaned toward me, over the bar between us.

"You have my hair, not your mother's. She was a pretty, fair child. But you have the hair of my mother and grandmother before me. You should let it grow, Meg. Long hair gives a person strength."

She laughed.

"Well," she said, "that's what my grandmother used to say."

Check In: The Ins and Outs of Inheritances

One of the connections we share as living beings is that we inherit qualities from our ancestors. What do you think you've inherited from your grandmother or your mother? From your grandfather or your father? Which qualities and characteristics are most important to you? Which influences you the most? What choices can you make in your life that your foremothers or forefathers didn't make or couldn't make? Would you make any of the same choices? What have you already discovered about being female that future generations may learn from you?

Changes and Moving On

In *Shizuko's Daughter*, by Kyoko Mori, the main character, Yuki, is growing up without her mother. When Yuki was twelve years old, her mother committed suicide. In this selection from the novel, it's years after her mother's death, and Yuki is talking with Mr. Kimura, who loved Yuki's mother when he and her mother were both young. He's now married to Yuki's aunt, Aya. Yuki tells him . . .

> *"I believe that if we could foresee the future, none of us would ever fall in love. It comes to nothing one way or the other."*
>
> *Mr. Kimura leaned back against the tree, his arms folded. He seemed to be thinking for a long time. Finally, he said, "When I was younger and my marriage was going badly, I used to think the same thing too. What's the point? It all turns out badly. I felt that way again when I heard about your mother's death. I was forty then. But in the last few years, as I've gotten to be forty-five and forty-six, I began to think differently. I think now that it's worth it all the same, loving someone. It may not turn out right, but I want to love someone in spite of it. In a way it means more because the odds are against us. If I didn't think that, I would never have married Aya."*
>
> *Yuki tried to imagine it—herself at forty-five feeling that love was worthwhile. It was difficult. All she could think of was herself running around the track, a fast lap, a slow lap, endlessly, while the others fell in love.*

Yuki's feelings about love change when her father gives her a sketchbook of her mother's that he has saved. It's filled with pictures in watercolor and pencil of Yuki and her father. Like your notebook and sketches, it is a vision of its creator's true self. As

Yuki looks through the pictures, she thinks again about love, her parents, and her future.

> *In the middle part of the sketchbook, Yuki saw sketch after sketch of herself done in pencil. The strokes were swift but careful. In the later pictures, she recognized some of the clothes, toys, places. . . .*
>
> *On the second-to-last page, Yuki found a detailed watercolor portrait of herself holding some daisies to her nose and smiling a big, frank smile. . . . This is how my mother saw me, she thought, such a happy child. . . . We were happy, Yuki thought; anybody could tell.*
>
> *She turned to the last page. It was a pencil sketch of her father sleeping on the chaise lounge in the cottage. Her mother's pencil strokes were at once bold and careful. She must have been eager to sketch him before he woke up. Several hydrangea blossoms had been pressed right onto the page. . . .*
>
> *(H)e looked slightly sullen but almost comical, endearing even. . . . This is how she wanted to see him, Yuki thought. . . . She even pressed these flowers to the last page of her sketchbook . . . . She must have loved him still.*
>
> *Yuki closed the sketchbook and put it on the bed. She wondered when her mother had stopped loving her father, what she would say if Yuki could ask her now, "Did you regret loving him?" Mr. Kimura had said . . . that he wanted to love someone even if it ended in sadness. . . . But love brings sadness, Yuki thought, even when the other person doesn't hurt you on purpose. . . .*
>
> *Yuki closed the sketchbook and held it on her lap. My mother, she thought, wanted to be . . . at the center of my mind, almost swallowed up by the light around it but always there. She would want me to look beyond her unhappiness.*

Family Expectations

How can Yuki do what she says her mother wants her to do, "to look beyond her [mother's] unhappiness?" What suggestions would you make to Yuki about her future? Most parents and daughters have expectations of each other. Have you ever tried to be different from your mother and/or your father? Have you ever tried to be the same as your mother and/or your father? What have you learned about being different from your parents and/or siblings?

What makes you happy when you think about growing up? Can you list your happiest expectations? Which expectations make you sad? What role has love—being loved or loving other people—played in either or both types of expectations?

The last story in this chapter is about a girl living in Europe who is unsure whether or not she can be her true self as a woman. In *Over the Water*, by Maude Casey, fourteen-year-old Mary Maeve calls her mother Mammy. Mary was born in London, and her mother, who is Irish Catholic, is very strict with her.

The family goes to Ireland to visit Mammy's farm and family. Life in the Irish countryside is confusing for Mary, who takes to her bed for days on end. Her aunt brings her a book of Irish folklore, about a nearby place called Tir Na N'Og, and the first Maeve, who was a queen. Mary struggles to understand why her mother named her Maeve after such a powerful woman at the same time that her mother doesn't seem to want her to be powerful.

When Mammy comes into the bedroom, I feel myself become tight all over. She fires desperate questions at me, so that my magic land recedes and her anxiety replaces it, clawing at me. When she pulls back the curtain and says, "It's a grand day!" I know that it's an accusation, and what she really means is, "Why aren't you out in the sunshine?"

She confuses me so much, with her code of words that mean different things from what they actually say. My head loses its lightness and clarity when I'm with her, so that I find myself hurtling words at her like cannonballs. And before I know where I am, I am struggling in tangled threads and I don't even know myself any longer what it is I'm trying to say. . . .

One morning, Mary Maeve decides to leave her room. It's early, and she sees a colt. As she gets closer to him, she decides she's going to ride him through the same forests the Maeve of Irish history lived in.

Shivering, I turn the colt back onto the track and continue toward the mountain. I am glad of the sun upon my back. I am glad of the warm moving body of the horse against my legs. What a shame it is that Mammy is afraid of horses. I wonder if she has ever walked this way? . . .

I am dreamy and spellbound. The elusive magic of Tir Na N'Og is all around me, and inside me, too. The whole land is alive with it. The cattle in the field beyond, lifting their heads as we pass, are like fairy cattle, belly-high in wild flowers and grasses. The mountain is changing color again. Two small wispy clouds are hanging gaily over its summit.

My belly is heavy and warm with my period. I clench and unclench my legs against the muscles of the colt. I am making my body work after so long. . . .

I am strong and calm. There is no distance between me and everything surrounding me. . . . There is no ending; everything is continuing. The whole land is alive, and the air above it. . . .

I have seen enough. I know now that it takes longer than an afternoon to reach a mountain. And that the land of your dreams might be the very one you're walking through. Curling my fingers in the tangle of his mane, I turn the colt back on himself and I head for home. . . .

I am luckier than any of the people who have gone before me. I do not have to work all my days in a numbing battle against poverty and sickness, in a struggle to bring up children in a world that denies them even food or warmth. I do not have to be a victim of circumstance. . . .

Yes, that's it! I have a choice. I do not have to be a victim of circumstances, of my parents' anger, or of anybody's expectations for me! I decided to take to my bed, and now I have decided to get up. I did that, and now I can decide to show them all that I am capable of making sensible decisions. The colt has come to no harm.

As we turn from the track and turn into the lane, I look back and say "Thank you." Then I see our house above the trees ahead of me. And as we start to trot down the lane, my heart is singing with its first real song of freedom.

Grown Up

This is a very beautiful description of a life-changing ride through the Irish countryside. Have you ever experienced anything so emotional that it made you feel as satisfied as Mary feels? What makes you feel free? How does your relationship with your parents affect your self-image or your self-confidence? Perhaps you can sketch or write about your moments of freedom. Freedom makes me think of my green stone, and of liking myself. What connections do you see between liking yourself and feeling free?

Mary's feeling of freedom could stay with her all her life. What predictions would you make for her when she's a woman? How do you feel about growing up? Talking to girls and women inside and outside your family about becoming women may inspire you to look forward to growing old and help you understand them. You may discover someone who took a chance and made her life better even when a tragic thing happened to her.

Now is a good time to reread your answers to the "Before and After" Check In questions at the beginning of this chapter. How and why would you change your answers to any of the questions? Which stories have you read that influenced you? What literature, movie, or art has influenced you in a powerful way? What do you think will stay with you into adulthood?

When you grow up, you'll be your true self as a grown-up. Remember Sandra Cisneros's description of what it means to be eleven? We have all the experiences and feelings of each year of our lives inside us. Everyone has positive and negative memories, and each of us can weave them into a rich life. What has happened to you is a part of whom you'll become, and your future shines like a green stone.

OUR TRUE SELVES

When I spend time with my true self I find out how powerful I am. —Sydelle

t's time for you to discover what a diverse group of girls and women think and feel about their true selves. They come from different countries, and among other places, they live in houses, huts, apartments, shelters, mansions, jails, and houseboats, and no matter where they are, each has a true self. Their words may help you think about what being a unique person—no matter how old you are—means to you. After reading this section, you will have an opportunity to write about who you are in that special place inside you.

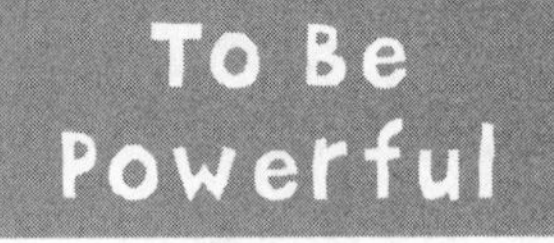

To Be Powerful

by Shakoiya, 11

I believe in speaking my mind and telling people what I feel and what I think and not to bite my tongue. What I mean is if someone is doing something to you, you should let them know about it before it gets worse. So always speak your mind, and that's when you're powerful. And never let any man or woman take advantage of you.

Inside Out

by Melissa, 17

My green stone is my sadness and hurt that I show everyone as anger.

An Adventurous Self

by Lesha, 12

My true self is taking a nap and doesn't want to be disturbed. But I can tell you how she is. She's adventurous and loves scary stuff.

My Green Stone

by Katie, 11

I think my true self is goofy and happy.

My True Self

by Joni, 13

I haven't found mine yet. She's very quiet, but she's in there. I can feel her.

Disappearing Acts

by Kizzy, 16

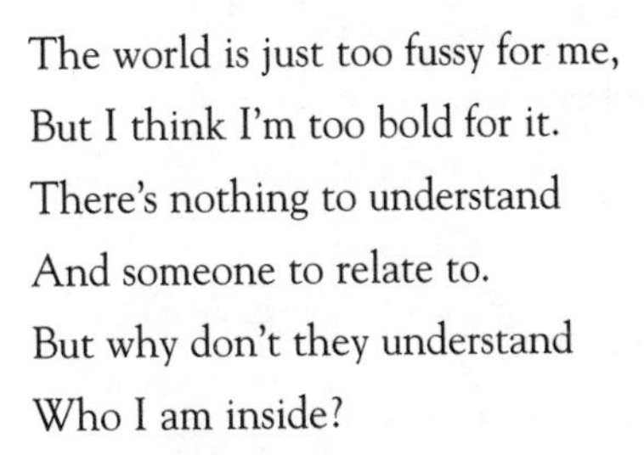

The world is just too fussy for me,
But I think I'm too bold for it.
There's nothing to understand
And someone to relate to.
But why don't they understand
Who I am inside?

The fact that I work hard at
everything
And I do all that I can
So they could comprehend.
There is no such thing as foolish
pride
For if there was then people would
Feel so empty
Trying to accomplish goals.
I see that I can't help so
I swallow up and disappear, for
I hate to be wrong or unwanted.
There's no one to hear my silent cries
Because no one was ever really
listening.

I had too much to say anyway
But then again nothing at all.
So while others act like they were
there
I turn around and disappear.

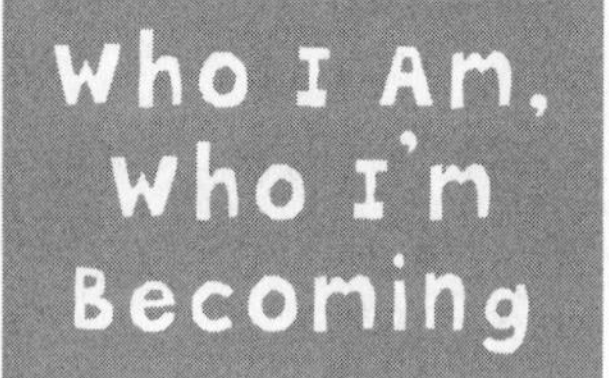

by Carolyn, 22

I believe that I am strong-willed and ambitious, destined to be powerful. Powerful to me means being myself and being happy with myself. I describe myself as intelligent, adventurous, and versatile. I strive to have a career and a family. I believe in being true to myself and living with no regrets. I find good in all.

In twenty-two years, I believe I have come full circle with certain aspects of my life, but there are many circles to be completed. My true self is capable of being child-like, but also grown-up and responsible. When necessary, I'm giving, caring, and sometimes even selfish. Being true means being honest even if it means admitting the negative and accepting what I can't change.

I wish I could be more open and express myself. Anger is easier to express than hurt and sadness. I'm trying to become someone who is more open. Although people say I can be stubborn, that's okay. Stubborn can be positive if it means keeping your own ideas and pursuing your dreams.

Being Reborn

by Rebecca, 46

I am going to be forty-seven years old, and I am being reborn. I am scared. I did what I was supposed to do: that was get married, have children, stay home, and take care of the house. But something went wrong, something that wasn't supposed to happen. Something I wasn't told could happen.

I was suddenly a widow, left with two children. I thought I was alone on this huge planet. But I am not alone. I have myself.

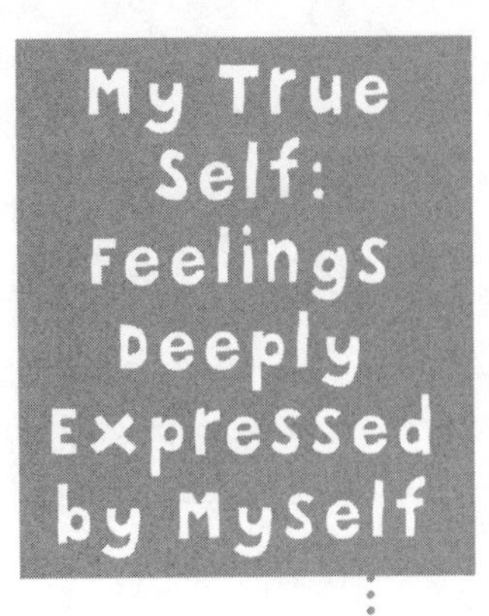

The real me inside is full of joy, love, and happiness. I'm full of love because you have to love yourself before you can love anyone else, and I love myself and everybody.

I'm filled with happiness because I'm happy with whatever I do to make myself happy. I'm filled with joy.

by Keosha, 12

My True Self

by Tammie, 33

I, Tammie, am a very special person in my own way. I love everybody regardless of color or who they are. I am a very loving and caring person who wants everything under the sun for my kids. My two girls are everything to me. I am down in a rut right now because I really love my husband, but he has a problem that I can't deal with. I have stood behind him for four years.

So now Tammie is ready to go on with her new life and enjoy her children and relax. Stop being that other person and stand up for herself.

My True Self

by Sibley, 26

My true self is a dappled green
light through a leafy canopy
limitless as water,
bright as stars.
But I keep forgetting that
and believe I'm tax returns
and back orders
and constant complaints,
that I'm dimples and
dented car fenders
and the annoying, funny
theme songs to TV sitcoms.
Sometimes I think
what I need to do,
rather than what I want to do.
I forget
in the face of fear,
that I am the face of love.
Just remembering
makes me cry
softly in forgiveness.

A Happy, Strong Self

by Gina, 15

My true self includes the fact
that I was raped and
that I didn't let it get it to me.
I'm still my happy, strong self
and I will never let it get me
down.

What Makes Me Feel Powerful

by Chernell, 9

When I get an A+ or an A on a test.
When I get told I am smart.
When people tell me I will become something big.
When people tell me I am strong-willed.
That's what makes me feel powerful.
Strong-willed is independent and brave.
And I'll stay like that forever.

My True Self

by Lydia, age 9⁷⁄₈

My true self just woke up from a loooonnngggg catnap. Now the reason I call it a catnap is because I believe I was always sorta awake. What do I mean by that? Well, when I get my feelings hurt, my true self tells me not to get mad at the person who hurt my feelings.

But today it really woke up. It turned me into a person who pretty much does what I want unless my mom tells me not to, then I try to be content without it. Good night, true self.

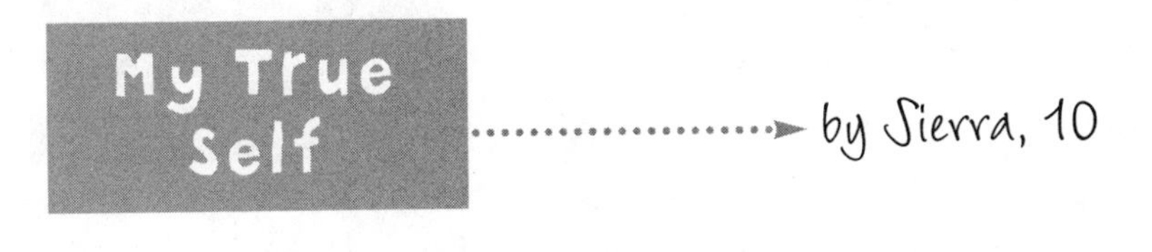

My true self is someone who cares and someone who helps. And is sweet and very interesting.

I show my inner self when something tragic happens and also when something that isn't tragic happens.

My true self really believes that I'm not embarrassed about my dyslexia because it's my true self.

I'm also very artistic and I like to paint stuff.

My True Self

by Lizzy, 10 3/4

A lot of people think one personality in you is who you really are. But I think, at least, my inner self is many personalities swirled together, to become me!

I think I have a great singer inside me, wanting to push out, let go—but somehow it's having a lot of trouble. . . . The reason, I think, that my inner-singer-self-person is having trouble getting out is that, when it's about to push through, I'm criticized. "You sing too loud!" "Stop singing, I'm trying to talk." "STOP singing, I'm trying to study!" over and over again.

My inner self is my family, my friend that I can trust. . . . My family's history. My history. MY inner self is ME!

by Melissa, 11

My true self is being generous. I enjoy giving things to other people. I also enjoy being by myself and just having time to think. I enjoy writing stories. Since I am very imaginative, I daydream a lot. I like to sit and pet my rabbit. I also like to read.

I am an artistic person; I love colors. I draw when I'm bored. I like to talk, although I am usually shy. I am sometimes what other people call "weird." I think I am a special person.

P.S. Hi, how are you? I am fine.

My True Self

by Carrie, 11

My true self is someone I can't really put my finger on, but I know I'm loving, caring, funny, and I'm really social. I can make friends with just about everyone and also always think ahead like what kind of shoes I'm going to wear to the prom or who I'm going to get married to sometime.

Wanting to know ahead is good. Other times it's bad. I want to be a lawyer, and I'm already starting to learn the things you have to learn. So far, I like it. . . .

Remembering

by Veronica, 17

My true self remembers me.
When women suffer
Too much because
You men ruined women's lives
A lot through the entire world.
That's a message for men
From my true self.

My True Self

by Brittany, 11½

I think my true self is a kind, loving, talkative person. I am a wonderful equestrian (horse rider). When I get on a horse, I can just *ride*! I'm never nervous; I just know inside that I can jump the three-foot jump.

I also have a wonderful memory. I can remember things from a long time ago. My inner self has a tendency to love animals. When I'm around them I feel so . . . great! It's like I become one when I'm around one. That's why when I grow up I want to be a veterinarian.

In addition, I love to draw horses or just anything else. Drawing always makes me feel so relaxed. . . .

My very last thing is that I love to shop. I'm always myself when I shop. I know where to go, and how to get there. I just love to shop—and talk.

My True Self

by Diana, 41

My true self's name is Dicey, which is my childhood name and the one all my friends use. As I got older, and entered the "professional" and adult world, I was encouraged to put away my childish things—this included the persona of Dicey.

But she still exists and when I need to be myself, I can always go where she is, and without too much effort, bring my true self out and really be the child-girl-woman I want to be.

My True Self

by Susan, 46

My true self hurts when anyone else hurts. What is difficult for me is to remember that people who lash out, are mean, cruel, or angry, are really hurting.

I'll cry at the drop of a hat when I hear music or see someone in pain. But I love to laugh, and nothing is more special than laughing so hard with your head thrown back and tears down your cheeks.

I cherish quiet, trees, peace, children, animals, and special parties when people are their true selves.

Planet Escapism

by Crystal, 16

My true self's name is Crystal. My true self does not want to grow up. Being an adult does not appeal to me. It's too complicated. Too much stuff to remember. Too much pressure. Yeah, that's it.

My true self likes simple things. Nothing complicated. Simple like childhood where everything is on your terms.

My true self hates change. My true self loves happiness, but isn't happy all of the time. My true self (contrary to popular beliefs) is very intelligent. My true self loves to be tickled. My true self loves little kids, but don't tell anyone. They may think the outside me is soft.

My true self likes to escape. To touch the sky on swings. . . .

Come.

Follow.

Line up.

You are all sheep.

"Not I!" said Crystal (the true self).

My Grace

by Elvie, 18

My true self is a safe place
It's where I get my grace
And it helps when I'm lost in a maze.

My true self is cool like mint
Deep inside.

My green stone is my heart.
It's sweeter than a Pop-Tart.

It's more valuable than any gem
It's prettier than anything else.

Who I Am

by Adeola, 16

I am a very sensitive person at times. Sometimes what people say to me can really mean a lot. I often sit by myself and think, really think about my life. When I think about me, I cry sometimes because it really shows that I really care about myself and actually worry about my future.

When I'm not by myself, I'm usually with my friends or my boyfriend. I like to talk about anything and like going anywhere. . . . If something really hits me or I am really deeply interested, that's when I speak out.

I find myself to be a caring person, and I am always there to listen. I don't really confide in anybody about anything. I usually keep things to myself. I haven't really found anyone I can trust enough with my feelings. I love myself though, and I love being the true me.

Finding Out Who I Am

by Elizabeth, 12

Today, I am strong. I almost feel like I could take on the world. I strive on strength. But also on caring and love. It just occurred to me that I am actually a strong woman. Yes, I do feel I am a woman now though I haven't gotten my period yet.

I do not feel you need your period to become a woman. That is usually the most important part. But to me it is simply physical. I am not saying that your period is not important in your life. It's just that it is not as important as most other things.

I feel that I have become a woman mentally. That I have found maturity without losing the part of me that I love. My imagination, my dreams, myself. I have made it all the way into eighth grade without becoming merely an object for the public. For that, I am special. I have seen many girls fall into that horrible fate. I know it will never happen to me. I am my very own special self. With my young girl still lovingly inside when I grow up and physically mature. I am different and strong, but special.

What I Feel My True Self Is

by Anisah, 16

I don't really know who my true self is at this point in my life. I'm young and in high school. Most of my waking hours are spent studying to get good grades and get a good scholarship so I can be somebody important (meaning professionally). I feel my true self is a person who is quiet and talkative, understanding and selfish; I'm tons of things, good and bad.

I feel that I listen to people's problems too much so that I don't really have time to think about me and only me.

When I'm by myself I feel like I should be doing something to help others. Sometimes I feel I am just going to burn out from listening to people. Not that I don't love the people, but what about me and my pain and my loneliness?

And before this day I never really thought about my true self. And now I feel I want to know and that I will take time to find out about who I am.

The Real Me

by Cara, 16

Crazy
Weird
Happy
Sad
Angry
Lonely
Friendly
Can party all night long
Listens to all types of music
Spiritual
All of these things make up the
Real Me.

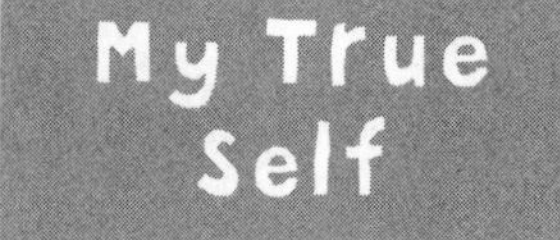

My True Self

by Nenee, 24

I don't believe I have just one true self. There are many, but I only know or am aware of but a few. Those few I can count on one hand.

For years I've known the self that motivates me to live life to the fullest, to fulfill my dreams. The self that everybody else needs, as well as myself. The self that is unstoppable and demanding.

Lately, the past month or so, I've encountered a self that I'm not too sure I like, but to some extent do like and appreciate because it is me. This self isn't so much a scared me, but the one that isn't as strong or powerful. In fact, it's weak and lonely. The side that isn't independent. The side that will latch on, latch onto someone I love. I'm not used to this self. And so, the self I've always been and lived by is in constant battle with its opposite.

What has occurred has taught me something. That my journey for self will not always be a pleasant one. But in the end, it will only (or so I hope) make me stronger . . . allow me to be only one—Nenee.

Who Am I?

by Cindy, 17

I really am not too sure. Sometimes I feel lost, and go crazy. Sometimes I just don't know if I am someone at all. My true self is very hidden. I may try to bring it out, but it is very hard for me. Sometimes thinking about myself makes me very sad, because I feel as if my life is falling apart. Everything seems so twisted and upside down for me.

I think I should start thinking about myself and stop thinking about other people, because they are not really thinking of me. Only I can think of myself, and only I know exactly who I am, nobody else.

The things that I think make me a young woman are my heart, mind, and body. These things control me, and build up my self-esteem, and help me to know who I am.

Last, but not least, I am sexy, sweet, honest, truthful, loving, caring, and sharing.

All these things are what make me who I am and a young, black, intelligent woman.

But I Wouldn't

by Christina, 12

When I wake up,
Well, I know I'm gonna be,
I'm gonna be the girl
Who wakes up free from drugs.
When I go out,
Yeah, I know I'm gonna be,
I'm gonna be the girl
Who walks away from drugs.
If I don't take them,
Yeah, I know I'm gonna be,
I'm gonna be the girl
Who's stronger than the rest.
But I wouldn't smoke any laced-up joint,
And I wouldn't do any other drug,
Just to be the kid who fits in with all the
Rest of
Those doped up kids.

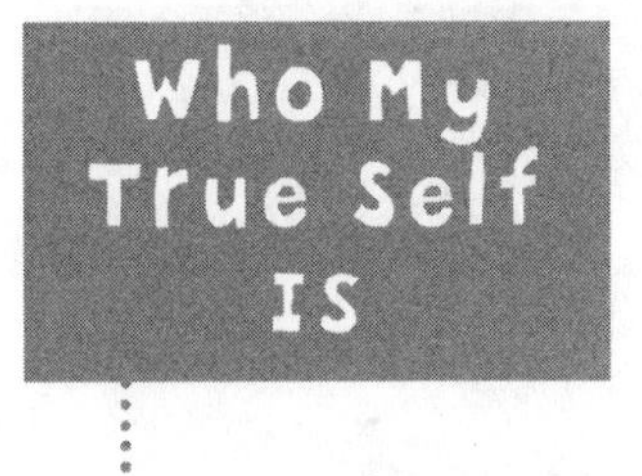

by Shaniqua, 16

My true self has not been totally developed yet. There is much I must strive to learn about who I really am. Day by day, when I think, I discover more of who I really am. Sometimes what I do one day contradicts what I might do another day. My self is like the seasons, always changing, never staying long enough to be caught.

Sometimes I think real hard to try to define who I am, what I stand for or what I believe. When I do this what happens is the things I encounter daily cloud the true image of who I am, what I am becoming, and what I'm trying to be.

I could give you a long definition of me. I could say "Shaniqua is like this and likes this," but am I really describing all the true attributes of me? Good with the bad? In reality, I'm still digging because there's something inside me, still trying to define itself.

What I am is a caterpillar in a cocoon or a baby in a womb or a coal under pressure. The end result will be true and beautiful, but now I'm in the metamorphic process. My life will center around reaching that point or goal within me. When I reach it, I'll stand tall and proud, expressing and delighting in my true self.

I really don't know, but I have some idea. I think that I'm a really nurturing person to others, but I don't express this on myself. I think I have a purpose on this earth, but I haven't quite figured it out yet. Maybe I'm not supposed to know yet, but it would be nice if I get some kind of sign.

It seems like I'm a nothing, meaningless, and empty. Like I'm supposed to help, or please others, but neglect myself. I also feel out of place, and lonely at times. Like no one understands me. I know I'm supposed to feel fortunate because I'm loved and have shelter, but there are other things that I need and want without being called selfish.

My True Self

by Kristina, 9

My true self is lonely, happy, sad, nice, mean, pretty, ugly, scared, surprised, and funny. When I say I'm ugly, it means I'm bad; pretty means I'm good.

And I am all of the words I said all the time at the same time. You may not know it, but deep down inside me I am.

Expressing Your True Self

Now it's time to find the words that describe you from the inside out. As you write in your notebook, welcome the words that come to you, and choose the ones that reveal what's deep inside you. It may take more than one try to express very deep feelings and ideas that are important to you. You are in charge. Write these words as a list or in paragraphs, in a circle or a spiral, or create whatever shape you choose. You may want to check in with what you write in your notebook to remind yourself of what makes you happy—and unique.

Think about the feelings you experience when you read your words and other girls' words about their true selves. Are you ready to express your true self? Have you found ways to be yourself that you would share? Some girls make promises to themselves to help them express their true selves at least once a day. In a workshop in Texas, we stood in a circle and each person made a promise. One girl said, "I'll always remember there are girls and women who'll be there for me." Another said, "I'll hold onto my dream no matter what happens." What promises would you make to your true self? Make a greeting card for yourself that celebrates the promises you are making.

For some of us, sharing a true self may come spontaneously, and for others it can be a process that takes time. That's part of being unique. What makes you feel safe sharing your true self? What scares you? Write a letter even if you decide not to mail it. Just writing your feelings down will help—and you can share it when you're ready. You'll know when it's the right time.

It's almost time to finish this book, and I'm feeling a little sad. I know when I look around a workshop—or right now, when I'm imagining you reading these words—I think about the strength and independence of all the girls I've met. It inspires me to be my best self and to have faith in the future. I'm so glad we've spent this time together.

Feeling Proud of Yourself

The last book we read is another picture book. It's called *Zora Hurston and the Chinaberry Tree*. The author is William Miller, and the pictures are watercolors painted by a husband-and-wife team, Ying-Hwa Hu and Cornelius Van Wright. The pictures are mostly in greens and browns, and the young Zora looks like a warm and lively young girl.

Zora Neale Hurston was a writer who wrote about her own people, the people she was proudest of, black Americans. She collected folklore about African-American life, and she wrote novels, short stories, and books of anthropology. (Anthropology is the study of people.) Zora traveled in the American South and collected stories told to her by black African-Americans as she passed through their towns. Alice Walker, author of *Finding the Green Stone*, said she "needed" Zora's writings because they told stories she hadn't found in literature before. They are universal, and all of us can learn from them.

Zora had a hard life as a writer. One of the reasons was because she used an unusual "voice" in her writing; the people in her books spoke like "ordinary" Southern black people instead of like the speech usually found in books. Zora used folk speech instead of standard English. Maybe you or someone you know speaks with an accent, in slang like hip-hop, or some other way that's different from most other people you know. Being different is challenging and, as Zora discovered, can also be rewarding.

There was something besides the language in Zora's work that people couldn't accept: that blacks are a proud and daring people who have survived their struggles in a patriarchy.

Zora died penniless in a welfare home in Florida. When Alice read that Zora's grave didn't have a marker on it, she went to Florida to do what felt like a "duty" to another black woman writer. In a cemetery overgrown with weeds, Alice found what she thought was Zora's grave. She had a headstone put on it that says:

ZORA NEALE HURSTON
"A GENIUS OF THE SOUTH"
NOVELIST FOLKLORIST
ANTHROPOLOGIST
1901–1960

Telling you this story about Alice and Zora brings together two women's voices that inspire us to be our true selves all our lives. Zora makes me believe, as she wrote in her novel *Their Eyes Are Watching God*, that I can wrap the horizon around me, and as Zora says, "the horizon is the biggest thing on this earth."

Zora spent her childhood in a small town called Eatonville, Florida, where her father was mayor. Eatonville was the first all-black, incorporated town in America, and she learned to have pride in her own people, which lasted all her life. From her mother, she also learned something very important—as you'll see.

In *Zora Hurston and the Chinaberry Tree*, Zora is a young girl looking for *her* voice:

Zora Hurston loved the chinaberry tree.

Her mother taught her to climb it, one
branch at a time.

From the tree, she could see as far
as the lake, as far as the horizon. . . .

Zora dreamed of seeing the cities beyond
the horizon, of living there one day.

But only boys fished in the lake,
only men traveled to the cities.
Zora watched with envy as the wagons
rattled down the dusty roads

Her father told her to wear a dress,
He warned her about girls who didn't obey
their fathers, girls who didn't grow up to be
young ladies.

But Zora only listened to her mother.

She taught Zora that everything had a voice:
the trees and rushing wind, the stars
in the midnight sky.

She taught Zora that the world belonged
to her, even the lake and far-off horizon.

So Zora went everywhere. . . .

She followed boys to the edge of campfires,
listened while other fathers sang about John Henry . . .

Zora learned about Africa, the place where
she and her people came from.

In Africa they had been kings and queens,
builders of cities that stood for thousands of years. . . .

One morning Zora's mother didn't feel well.
She told Zora not to worry . . .
She told Zora to go
outside and play, to climb her favorite tree.

But Zora couldn't play. She saw how tired
her mother was . . .
Day after day, Zora sat beside her mother's bed
telling her the stories she had heard
beside the campfires.

Her mother smiled and asked Zora to always
remember what she had learned.

Stories, she said, kept their people alive.
As long as they were told, Africa would live
in their hearts.
Zora promised to remember.

Zora's mother slowly got worse.
Men and women came to sit up with her
through the long, hot nights. . . .

Zora was sitting in the parlor when her
father told her she would not see her
mother again.

Zora felt as if she had died. She watched while the old
people stopped the clocks, put sheets on the mirror.

She watched while the women cried and the men
stared at their Sunday shoes.
But then she could sit still no more.

Zora ran from the house, ran all the way
to the chinaberry tree.

[Zora] climbed the first branch and the next,
climbed almost to the top.

A sparrow sang to her in a voice like her
mother's. The sparrow told her
not to give up, to climb even higher.

From the top of the tree Zora saw again
the world her mother had given her:
the lake filled with fish, the cities where she would
tell people all she had learned . . .

Zora promised her mother that she would
never stop climbing,
would always reach for the newborn sky,
always jump at the morning sun!

A mother's illness and death can be devastating events, yet Zora and Yuki, the character whose mother killed herself, find ways to take care of themselves. Did you guess Zora was going to the chinaberry tree? Is there a special place you and a family member or someone else you love can share? Is there any place you look forward to as an escape or where you go to comfort yourself? Maybe you could write about or sketch your special place and what you find there. In some ways, a true self is like a cherished retreat or a source of power. How do you feel about this idea?

Your Voice Is Your Power

Our closing discussion in Girls Speak Out is about the power of each person to make a difference. Each voice we've encountered, whether it's our own voice, another girl's or woman's voice, live or from literature, is special.

Each voice matters.

How will you use the information in this book? Will you organize Girls Speak Out workshops or a club? Will you continue to write and draw about your inner life? How do you feel about showing your notebook to other people, or maybe one day publishing it? Describe what has changed in you after reading this book.

Doing Girls Speak Out workshops and writing this book encouraged me to ask and answer some questions about my own girlhood. When I started over a decade ago, I spent the first two years exploring the good and bad things I had experienced while growing up. It might be helpful for you to know that I discovered, when I looked deep inside myself, that there was no secret "waiting to get me." I used to think I had something inside me I was ashamed of or that wasn't as good as other people. Some of the girls who wrote about their true selves had a similar feeling.

Now I've found my true self, and I'm glad I can be who I always wanted to be. And it's wonderful that being my true self connects me with girls like you. I am certain that you can be happy no matter what happens if you know and trust your true self.

When we created Girls Speak Out, Gloria and I knew we had lost parts of our true selves as we were growing up. We tried to make things better for other people, especially girls and women, but sometimes we got out of balance by paying more attention to other people than to ourselves. Each of us found our true selves again when we were in our early fifties. So you see, it's never too late.

But when we were your age, there wasn't a Girls' Movement or a Women's Movement to let us know that the patriarchy was the problem, not us.

Now, you don't have to grow up feeling there's something wrong with you. Or that you're the only one who feels the way you do.

We know that girls can resist losing their true selves as they grow up.

You can be your true self all your life.

Promises

Why do you think girls in workshops want to make promises to themselves? What promise would you make to yourself? To your mother or father? Do you think it was important for Zora to climb, even after her mother's death? How would you describe Zora's true self? Write a note to Zora about her mother's death in which you describe a valuable gift she left for Zora.

Which person in your life has a true self that's openly expressed? Who hides their true self? Perhaps there's a story or girl's writing in this book or in your notebook that you could share with someone you care about, which might help that person express and hold onto a true self. Make a section in your notebook of what you can share with friends, family, and others. You're becoming a teacher, that is, someone who passes on what you and others have learned to many people.

Closings and Beginnings

Being who I am makes
me truly happy. —*Graça*

Now you have a notebook of your writings and memories. When you close this book, you'll have new memories, too.

We can't see our true selves, just as we can't see each other right now. Like words, our true selves touch and connect us even when we're not in the same room.

We'll be together each time we remember how strong and independent each girl and woman is. When we see a green stone in our imagination or in our hand, we will be looking at a symbol of each of us, a unique combination of our ancestors, our families, and ourselves.

If we were together in the same room, we'd play the Tunnels game, giving each other permission to go.

We'd go out the door laughing and hugging each other. I'd watch the last girl leave as I pack my books and papers.

But . . .

You and I met in these pages. We don't have to say good-bye the way we would in person.

Let's try this final Check In.

As you end this book, think about your green stone. Think about all the green stones shining inside girls and women. Now . . . please read the words below. I hope they make you smile, too.

Our green stones remind us we can do things no one else can,
Because we're each unique and special,
But we're all connected to each other
And to the biggest green stone of all:
The Earth.

Welcome to Girls Speak Out.

About the Ancient Artifacts

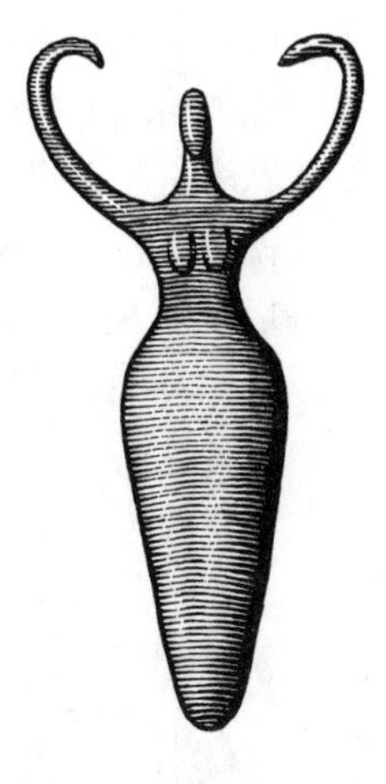

1. This Nile River goddess is an inside-out image to a lot of girls because her arms resemble Fallopian tubes (the part of our reproductive systems that carries eggs to the uterus, where they're either fertilized [and a pregnancy begins] or they're discharged during a period). This goddess is an ancient African symbol of an overflowing female body and spirit.

2. The Cretan Snake Goddess was found in a palace on Crete, a Greek island that is an equal distance between Europe and Africa. She's about 3,900 years old, and it's believed that she understood the snake, a powerful image of rebirth that sheds its skin.

3. The Willendorf Goddess is approximately thirty thousand years old, and she was found all over Europe. She's one of the oldest sculptures of a human, and she was designed to be handheld or placed in the ground to stand.

4. When girls hold this ancient Greek figure, they often have the same idea: she looks like a "cramps doll" because of the position of her hands and knees. She's about four hundred years old and was found in tombs.

5. Approximately six thousand years old, this image of a dreaming woman was found on an island in the Mediterranean. Some believe that a Neolithic (Stone Age) goddess culture was practiced in the caves where she was found, and that they found their wisdom in dreams.

6. Kuan Yin is an ancient Chinese goddess who reminds us that peace comes from the inside out. She is a thinker known for her compassion and forgiveness.

7. This gentle figure, who seems wrapped up in herself, stands upright, and her arms extend into snakelike coils that wrap around her body. She is a European statue, and her face's lack of features reminds us that all females have a lot in common.

8. This woman is a European crone goddess. A crone is an old wise woman. Old age is a time of power. She, too, understands the snake.

9. This is an Eskimo image that faces in two directions. Some believe that the bowl-like surface was used like a candle, as a place where things were burned to celebrate an important event.

10. This African image is made from wood and is a popular female figure. It is believed that she was carried by women who wanted to have children, as well as by women who didn't want to bear children, but they would carry—and dance with—the figure in place of children.

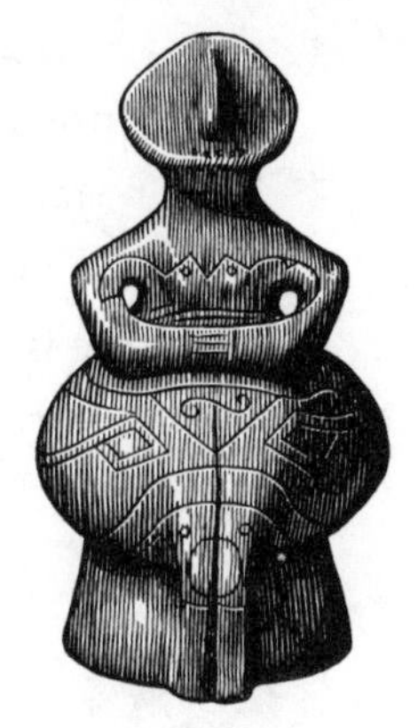

11. This figure appears to be seated on a throne, but it's really her body that resembles a throne. She's thought to symbolize Mother Earth. This artifact is approximately forty-five hundred years old. She is European.

12. This tiny figure is European and is called a votive figure, something offered in prayer. Thousands like her have been found. She, too, fits easily in a hand, but she also stands upright, and statues like her were found standing all around ancient rooms.

13. This is a piece of a wall carving that is thought to be European. The goddess is carved with animals, and she is holding symbols of the harvest. Ancient images of females were often associated with life, including the earth's gift of other forms of life.

.... Guide to Girls Speak Out Workshop Participation

You can experience Girls Speak Out workshops in many different ways.

1. Check out the Girls Speak Out website (*www.girlsspeakout.org*) or use the contact information listed in the introduction to this book to find out if and when workshops are scheduled in your neighborhood. You will also find the names and locations of certified Girls Speak Out leaders or trainers.

2. Contact Andrea and arrange to have her lead Girls Speak Out workshops in your neighborhood.

3. Ask a school, club, or girls' organization that you know to contact Girls Speak Out to find out about hosting Girls Speak Out workshops.

4. Arrange for a training session for you or other girls and women to be certified (see an explanation below) to organize and lead Girls Speak Out workshops near you.

What Is Girls Speak Out Certification?

One of the important things Girls Speak Out shares with readers and workshop participants is trust. Each person who is with you as part of Girls Speak Out must be worthy of your trust. Each person must understand the importance of what is included in this book and be able to help even after the workshop ends. For instance, sometimes a girl will talk or write about a serious issue that she can't or shouldn't handle alone. Girls Speak Out representatives are trained to help her.

To make sure this follow-up happens, and in order to use the Girls Speak Out name, girls and women who want to organize and lead workshops must be qualified. You'll know they're qualified if they have gone through a series of steps that is called Girls Speak Out Certification Training. Certification can be done in person or long distance.

Here is a snapshot of the process for certification:

1. Read *Girls Speak Out: Finding Your True Self.*

2. Contact Girls Speak Out to register for a handbook and training materials for a pilot program.

3. After receiving your training materials, recruit girls and women as participants in a pilot program, and submit your list to Girls Speak Out.

4. Following the handbook, hold a session training for women participants that lasts approximately four hours.

5. Organize two Girls Speak Out workshops with approximately fifteen to twenty diverse girls aged nine to sixteen years and three to five women participants of various ages. Hold the workshops from 10 A.M. to 4 P.M. the first day and from 10 A.M to 2 P.M. the second day. Together, these two workshops complete a Girls Speak Out program.

6. Hold a two-hour debriefing immediately after the second workshop for adult participants to identify girls who need further support and to analyze feedback from the girls who attended the program.

7. Schedule a follow-up meeting for at least two hours to evaluate leaders and trainees.

8. Submit evaluations in writing to Girls Speak Out for review.

9. Certificates are evaluated every two years.

Here is the table of contents for the Girls Speak Out Training Handbook:

Overview of the Girls Speak Out Program
Purpose and Method of Training
Training Workshop Objectives
How to Recruit Participants: Standards and Techniques
Finding Support from Donors
Overview of Training Time
Training Agenda
Program Supplies and Costs
Girls Speak Out Workshops' Agenda
Girls Speak Out Follow-Up Guidelines
Evaluations
Certification and Renewal

If you have any questions, please contact me. I look forward to hearing about your experiences with Girls Speak Out.

.... First National Girls' Conference: Girls Global Plan of Action

The words in the Girls USA Plan of Action come from the girls themselves, with changes made only for clarity and to avoid repetition. There is no copyright on it, which means you can use it without asking permission.

A Global Model

First National Girls' Conference Cosponsors: National Girls' Coalition and the United States Committee for UNICEF:

Members of the National Girls' Coalition Girls Steering Committee: Lauren Bernardo, Betty Boo, Colette Coleman, Christina Dry, Elizabeth Foster-Shaner, Callie Garnett, Jean Garnett, Margie Gonzalez, Mavis Gruver, Maya-Halona Walker, Lizzy Hazlett, Clara Hess-Rhoades, Nia Kelly, Joanne Levine, Lisa Mathai-Davis, Tara Mathai-Davis, Marta Ostrovich, Sydelle Outing, and Sierra Templeton.

Members of the National Girls' Coalition: Convenor, Andrea Johnston; American Association of University Women, Jane Fonda, Girl Scouts of the USA, Girls International Forum, "Girls Speak Out," Global Kids, Inc., Milly Lee, Ms. Foundation for Women/Take Our Daughters to Work®, National Girls' Coalition Girls Steering Committee, *New Moon Magazine*, New York City Housing Authority, Nontraditional Employment for Women,

PC Girls, Planned Parenthood of New York City, Gloria Steinem, Marlo Thomas, and the YWCA of the USA.

Confronting Violence against Girls

Violence against Girls Is All around Us

Girls should be safe wherever we are and not be intimidated. We know about violence because it's something we see and feel. You can't be too young or too old to know violence can happen to you, and that it's not your fault. We need to understand that sexual abuse of children, for example, is bad and wrong, not just gross.

Violence is about power and control. It makes us feel isolated and alone, and it also makes us want to protect ourselves. We each experience some kind of violence in our lives: it can be emotional (treated like we're invisible or sexually harassed), physical (being hit), mental (being made fun of), or economic (living below the poverty line), or it can seem self-inflicted like anorexia and bulimia. It can happen in our homes (domestic violence), at school, on the streets, and wherever we go. Violence is unwanted and unnecessary. People who commit violent acts rationalize them so they don't have to admit they are wrong even though a girl could be hurt for life.

What Happens to Girls

Some girls are abused even though all of us (including girls who live in other countries) have the right to be respected by everyone. We can stand up for ourselves. It's important that we tell what's happening to us. We have the right to tell someone we trust.

There must be more use of positive reinforcement like praise and thanks. Parents should be responsible, and there should be parenting lessons. They should acknowledge that being a parent is a privilege and not a right. We know that when you have problems as a girl, you could still have them as an adult unless you talk and do something about them. Violence against girls isn't taken seriously even though it's hurtful, degrading, and harmful to us. When we see a girl who's badly neglected, for example, it makes us very sad and angry that she isn't protected. Girls should not be scared and in pain.

Girls should be in safe and supportive environments. We need to be respected as human beings.

What Girls Can Do to Be Safe

1. Don't accept violence; speak out about it and stand up against it.

2. Inform all girls of their right not to be violated at any age; teach girls about abuse early, and about letting someone know if it happens to them.

3. Provide knowledge of help and resources to all girls.

4. Find or create support groups and female self-defense classes in our home communities.

5. Organize peer support groups for victims of rape and abuse, and ask abuse victims who are girls to teach and run these groups.

6. Take home the information we learned at the First National Girls' Conference and have mini-conferences in our states.

7. Get the media involved in something positive like educating girls about violence for a change.

8. Sometimes one action can lead to others; for example, telling about a teacher touching you in a way that feels uncomfortable can encourage other girls to speak out.

9. Create and use networks of girls to spread stories of girls who successfully fought the system and overcame violence.
10. "Girlcott" products that promote violence.
11. Have self-esteem classes taught in schools as a subject like math and science.
12. Use peaceful resistance like Rosa Parks and Sojourner Truth did.

Girls' Rights Are Human Rights

Girls are individuals with natural rights equal to those of other humans. Girls are organizing a Girls' Movement that celebrates the right to be ourselves, and we're speaking out about unfairness. We are determined to change negative assumptions and stereotypes about girls. We want to change traditional roles for girls that are sexist, racist, classist, and ageist and encourage nontraditional roles that allow more choices and our right to be ourselves.

We are making history—*herstory*. We know females have been erased from history for being powerful, but we will stand up for what we believe in even if we stand alone. We will include boys, women, and men at different times because we know that in order to make the world a better place for girls we have to include all of us.

Our motto is: "Don't deal with it. Change it!"

Girls have the right to:

1. be who we are all the time
2. stay who we are all our lives
3. not be shunned because of our background
4. enjoy a safe environment
5. be president

6. choose whether to have children or not, including contraception, abortion, and good medical care for mothers and children
7. love whomever we want
8. be listened to
9. be free
10. be equal
11. stand up for ourselves
12. control our physical, emotional, intellectual, and sexual selves
13. say "no"
14. say "yes"
15. the same opportunities as boys wherever we are
16. enter any career we choose
17. be heard without age discrimination
18. be self-confident
19. travel
20. an education
21. buy and inherit property
22. learn about history without gender, race, and age bias
23. disagree
24. feel safe
25. be religious or nonreligious or not sure
26. optimum health
27. urge government to ratify (approve) girls' and children's rights
28. have the choice of coeducation or single-sex schools for girls
29. change old rules and customs that aren't fair
30. single-parent families, extended families, multi-parent families; whatever our families look like
31. be happy
32. love

33. make these rights public
34. be on school boards and boards of organizations dealing with girls' issues
35. food, shelter, and basic needs like water and clothes
36. medical research on health problems of girls
37. use all the rights we already have
38. YELL!
39. live

Images of Girls in the Media

The Reality

The media should offer truthful, positive role models for girls, and we should not be exploited and misrepresented by the media. We are physically diverse, coming in all shapes and sizes and from different cultures, races, and classes, with different abilities and sexual orientations.

How Images in the Media Affect Girls

Most images of girls in the media are stereotypes. Girls are often portrayed as skinny and white, as possessions and weak. Girls in the media are judged by their looks, and they're not interesting.

Our spirituality is left out. Media images can affect a girl's subconscious. Sometimes images of girls in the media control girls' lives, and they don't know it. For example, some girls feel they must diet in order to be beautiful, and they become anorexic and bulimic.

Girls should feel free to look however they want and be who they are. The goal is to have more realistic images of girls in the media.

Girls Can Be Heard

We can support what's positive. We need to start awareness early for boys and girls and teach gender equity ourselves.

How to change images of girls in the media:

1. Be public about our negative feelings about the media.
2. Be public about the positive things we can do.
3. Tell women they shouldn't accept unfair portrayals, either.
4. Support girls with different body shapes and sizes.
5. Don't watch or buy what's negative toward girls and/or women.
6. Put warning stickers on untruthful, anti-girl products.
7. Encourage ads that don't use females as objects.
8. Ask advertisers to have normal-looking people doing realistic things.
9. Don't Stop! Be Heard!!

Annotated Further Reading for Girls Ages Ten and Up

Compiled by Milly Lee, author and librarian

Allende, Isabel. *House of Spirits.* HarperCollins, 1985; *Daughter of Fortune.* HarperCollins, 1999; *Portrait in Sepia.* HarperCollins, 2001. Magical spiritualism and political and social history of some adventurous girls and women.

Alvarez, Julia. *How the Garcia Girls Lost Their Accents.* Algonquin, 1991. Latina girls growing up funny, and serious.

Angelou, Maya. *Know Why the Caged Bird Sings.* Bantam, 1969. A powerful story of hard times and survival in an award-winning autobiography.

Ashby, Ruth, and Deborah Gore Ohrn, ed. *Herstory: Women Who Changed the World.* Viking, 1995. Inspirational words from those who reclaimed women's history.

Atwood, Margaret. *The Handmaid's Tale.* Doubleday, 1990; *Robber Bride.* Doubleday, 1993. Strong girls who challenged their oppressors.

Avi. *The True Confessions of Charlotte Doyle.* Orchard, 1990. Newberry award-winning story of a thirteen-year-old girl at sea who uses her wits to survive. Avi's other titles are highly recommended as well.

Beales, Melba. *Warriors Don't Cry.* Pocket, 1995. The true story of the girl who integrated a school in the South.

Carroll, Rebecca. *Sugar in the Raw: Voices of Young Black Girls in America.* Crown Trade Paperbacks, 1997. Interviews that explore young black girls' attitudes.

Choi, Sook Nyul. *Year of Impossible Goodbyes.* Houghton Mifflin, 1991. A North Korean girl trapped in an occupied country.

Cleary, Beverly. *Girl from Yamhill: A Memoir.* Morrow, 1988. The true story of a beloved author's childhood. Read her other titles, especially the Ramona stories.

Coleman, Penny. *Rosie the Riveter.* Crown, 1995; *Fannie Lou Hamer and the Fight for the Vote.* Millbrook, 1993; *Mother Jones and the March of the Mill Children.* Millbrook, 1994. Photos and inspiring stories of women who stood up, took risks, and wrought changes.

Coles, Robert. *The Story of Ruby Bridges.* Scholastic, 1995. The poignant story of the only African-American child in her school in 1960.

Conway, Jill Kerr. *Written by Herself.* Vintage, 1990; *Road from Coorain.* Vintage, 1990. Autobiographies of a remarkable Australian woman who became the president of a renowned women's college in America.

Creech, Sharon. *Walk Two Moons.* HarperCollins, 1994. Newberry award-winning story of a thirteen-year-old Native American girl's search for her missing mother. All the titles of this author are recommended.

Crew, Linda. *Children of the River.* Delacorte, 1989. Story of a girl who fled Cambodia, then struggles to fit into America.

Cushman, Karen. *Catherine Called Birdy*. Clarion, 1994; *The Midwife's Apprentice*. Clarion, 1995; *The Ballad of Lucy Whipple*. Clarion, 1996. Engrossing tales of girls living in medieval times; Lucy Whipple was a spunky girl who came to California during the Gold Rush.

Divakaruvi, Chita. *Mistress of Spices*. Anchor/Doubleday, 1997. A mysterious Indian woman doles out spices and remedies in her new country.

Dorris, Michael. *Morning Girl*. Hyperion, 1992. A gentle sister and brother live in a tropical paradise.

Farmer, Nancy. *The Ear, The Eye and The Arm*. Orchard, 1994; *A Girl Named Disaster*. Orchard, 1996. Framer's imaginative works have won the Newberry Award, the National Book Award, and the Printz Award.

Frank, Anne. *The Diary of a Young Girl*. Doubleday, 1995. A timeless World War II story of growing up while hiding from the Nazis.

Freedman, Russell. *Eleanor Roosevelt: A Life of Discovery*. Clarion, 1993. The inspiring story of a shy young woman who became the First Lady of the USA.

Furlong, Monica. *Wise Child*. Random, 1987; *Juniper*. Knopf, 1991. Growing up female in Britain during the Dark Ages, a time when women healers faced prosecution.

Garden, Nancy. *Annie on My Mind*. Farrar, Straus and Giroux, 1982. Still being challenged, and still an excellent story of two teenagers who fell in love.

George, Jean Craighead. *Julie of the Wolves*. Harper, 1972; HarperCollins, 1994. Survival story of a remarkable Inuit girl growing up in the frigid north.

Hamilton, Virginia. *Sweet Whispers, Brother Rush*. Putnam,1982. A teenager resents taking care of her retarded brother. Read other stories by this excellent award-winning African-American author.

Hesse, Karen. *Letters from Rifka*. Holt, 1992. A young Jewish girl's story of coming to the USA from the Ukraine.

Houston, Jeanne Wakatsuki. *Farewell to Manzanar*. Bantam, 1973. A moving story of a Japanese family's victory over racism during World War II in an internment camp.

Hurston, Zora Neale. *Their Eyes Were Watching God*. HarperCollins, 1990. Love among people in folk speech.

Jenkins, Lyll Becerra de. *The Honorable Prison*. Dutton, 1988. A true story of survival during South African political turmoil.

Jiang, Ji Li. *Red Scarf Girl*. HarperCollins, 1997. An autobiography about growing up during the Chinese Cultural Revolution.

Kingston, Maxine Hong. *The Woman Warrior*. Vintage, 1989. Painful growing up while female, Chinese, and smart in a small central California town.

Lee, Milly. *Nim and the War Effort*. Farrar, Straus and Giroux, 1997. A young Chinese-American girl living in San Francisco's Chinatown helps her country and her family start a new tradition.

Levine, Gail Carson. *Ella Enchanted*. HarperCollins, 2003. A different twist to the Cinderella story; now made into a movie.

Levinson, Nancy Smiler. *She's Been Working on the Railroad*. Lodestar, 1997. Women built railroads, too.

Lowry, Lois. *Number the Stars*. Houghton Mifflin, 1989. Thrilling story of a ten-year-old girl being smuggled out of Nazi Germany.

Lyons, Mary. *Letters from a Slave Girl*. Scribner, 1992; *Sorrow's Kitchen*. Macmillan, 1990. Stories of escaping from slavery based on Harriet Jacob's autobiography.

Macy, Sue. *Winning Ways: A Photohistory of American Women in Sports*. Holt, 1996. The stories of the amazing physical strength and endurance of females.

Malone, Mary. *Maya Lin: Architect and Artist*. Enslow, 1995. The early life of the architect of, among other structures, the Vietnam War Memorial in the USA.

McCunn, Ruthanne Lum. *Thousand Pieces of Gold*. Beacon, 2004; *Moon Pearl*. Beacon, 2000. Two stories of very independent Chinese women who prevailed despite adversity.

Morrison, Toni. *Beloved*. Knopf, 1987. A very powerful story for older readers about overcoming the stigma of slavery.

Munoz-Ryan, Pam. *Riding Freedom*. Scholastic, 1998; *Esperanza Rising*. Scholastic, 2000. Both award-winning California stories, one of a stagecoach driver who isn't what others believed, and the other about a rich young girl who had to give up much to learn to survive as a migrant worker.

Nafisi, Azar. *Reading Lolita in Tehran: A Memoir in Books*. Random, 2003. Books brought together a group of women who supported each other while living dangerously in Iran.

Namioka, Lensey. *Ties That Bind, Ties That Break*. Delacorte, 1999. Going against her culture, a young Chinese girl refuses to have her feet bound and she suffered the consequences of her choice.

Nye, Naomi Shihab. *Habibi*. Simon & Schuster, 1997. A love story of a Palestinian girl and an Israeli boy.

Parks, Rosa, and James Haskin. *Rosa Parks: My Story*. Dial, 1992. The woman who refused to move to the back of the bus because she was black sparked a civil rights movement.

Paterson, Katherine. *Lyddie*. Lodestar, 1991; *The Great Gilly Hopkins*. Crowell, 1978. The story of girls working hard to free themselves from their miserable lives as mill girls.

Peck, Richard. A *Long Way from Chicago*. Dial, 1998; *A Year Down Yonder*. Dial, 2000. Newberry award-winning stories of Grandma Dowdel's amusing take on life.

Pettit, Jayne. *Maya Angelou: Journey of the Heart*. Lodestar, 1996. The acclaimed poet's struggles to find expression through her writing.

Rappaport, Doreen. *Living Dangerously*. HarperCollins, 1991. Stories of six strong American women who led daredevil lives while challenging limits.

Rinaldi, Ann. *A Ride into Morning: The Story of Tempe Wick*. Harcourt, 1991. The courageous story of fourteen-year-old Tempe Wick during the American Revolutionary War.

Rylant, Cynthia. *Missing May*. Orchard, 1992. Summer's beloved aunt dies, and she and her uncle struggle until a young boy comes into their lives.

San Souci, Robert. *Cut from the Same Cloth: American Women of Myth, Legend, and Tall Tales*. Philomel, 1993. Extraordinary folk tales from diverse American cultures.

Tan, Amy. *The Joy Luck Club*. Putnam, 1989; *The Bonesetter's Daughter*. Putnam, 2001. Stories of a Chinese-American family and their spiritual and cultural ties.

Temple, Frances. *The Ramsay Scallop.* Orchard, 1994. A young thirteenth-century girl goes on a pilgrimage.

Thomas, Marlo. *Free to Be . . .* Running Press Book Publishers, 2002. The first of a series of landmark books showing the importance of and fun in celebrating yourself.

Tsukiyama, Gail. *Women of the Silk.* St. Martin's Press, 1991. Chinese women were able to maintain their independence by working in the silk industry.

Walker, Alice. *In Search of Our Mother's Gardens.* Harcourt, 1983; *The Color Purple.* Harcourt, 1982. Stories of the richness of life despite poverty, slavery, and prejudice.

Wong, Jade Snow. *Fifth Chinese Daughter.* University of Washington Press, 1990. The first novel to depict home life in San Francisco's Chinatown as experienced by a young girl who grew up to be an award-winning author and ceramic artist.

Yang, Erche Namu. *Leaving Mother Lake: A Girlhood at the Edge of the World.* Little, 2003. Singer Namu sheds light on the unique matriarchal and matrilineal Moso culture of one of China's minority people.

Additional titles can be found in *Once Upon a Heroine* by Alison Cooper-Mullin and Jennifer Marmaduke Coye (Contemporary Books, 1999) and Shirleen Dodson's *100 Books for Girls to Grow On* (Harper, 1998).

Further Acknowledgments

The author gratefully acknowledges the Girls Speak Out program participants and the girls and women who read the first edition, whose words appear throughout this book.

Excerpt on page 43 from the introduction to *Wonder Woman* by Gloria Steinem. Copyright © 1995 by DC Comics. Reprinted by permission of DC Comics.

Excerpt on page 46 from *Outrageous Acts and Everyday Rebellions*, copyright © 1983 by Gloria Steinem. Reprinted by permission of the author.

Excerpt on pages 28–32 from *Women Hollering Creek and Other Stories*, copyright © 1991 by Sandra Cisneros. Reprinted by permission of Susan Bergholz Literary Agency.

Excerpt on pages 48–49 from *Brown Girl, Brownstones*, copyright © 1981 by Paule Marshall. Reprinted by permission of the Feminist Press.

Excerpt on pages 78–80 from *Sojourner Truth: Ain't I a Woman?*, copyright © 1992 by Patricia C. McKissack and Frederick L. McKissack. Reprinted by permission of Scholastic Press.

Excerpt on pages 92–95 and pages 96–99 from *Make Lemonade*, copyright © 1993 by Virginia Euwer Wolff. Reprinted by permission of Henry Holt and Company, Inc.

Excerpt on pages 112–116 from *Finding the Green Stone*, copyright © 1991 by Alice Walker and Catherine Deeter. Reprinted by permission of Harcourt Brace and Company.

Excerpt on pages 127–129 from *Ellen Foster*, copyright © 1987 by Kaye Gibbons. Reprinted by permission of Algonquin Books of Chapel Hill, a division of Workman Publishing.

Excerpt on pages 142–143 and pages 146–148 from *When I Was Puerto Rican*, copyright © 1993 by Esmeralda Santiago. Reprinted by permission of Addison Wesley Publishers Inc.

Excerpt on pages 162–166 from *Little Jordan*, copyright © 1995 by Marly Youmans. Reprinted by permission of David R. Godine, Publisher, Inc.

Excerpt on pages 166–170 from *Shizuko's Daughter*, copyright © 1993 by Kyoko Mori. Reprinted by permission of Henry Holt and Company, Inc.

Excerpt on pages 169-170 from *Over the Water*, copyright © 1993 by Maude Casey. Reprinted by permission of Henry Holt and Company, Inc.

Excerpt on pages 193-196 from *Zora Hurston and the Chinaberry Tree*, copyright © 1994 by William Miller. Reprinted by permission of Lee and Low Books, Inc.

About the Author

In 1994, after graduating from law school and blowing the whistle on a fellow teacher who was sexually harassing students, Andrea Johnston left thirty years of public and private school teaching in New York and California to cofound Girls Speak Out with Gloria Steinem. Andrea began traveling the country for what would be a three-year, fifteen-state, multiple-country odyssey resulting in the first edition of *Girls Speak Out: Finding Your True Self*, published in 1997 by Scholastic. Along the way, Andrea adapted the Girls Speak Out program for boys and coed groups.

In venues that ranged from public housing developments, living rooms, and classrooms to the CNN Center, the American Museum of Natural History, and the United Nations, Andrea learned firsthand about the misinformation children worldwide collect about gender. In January 1997, Andrea and Gloria helped organize the First National Girls' Conference at UNICEF House in New York City, which focused on media, violence, and girls' rights. Her Girls Speak Out Action Network grew to include girls from many continents as Andrea traveled as a speaker and to give workshops. In 2002 and 2003, she wrote a newspaper column for Filipina girls and was part of a task force in San Francisco that created a model Secure House for girl runaways. In 2003, she was named one of Fiji's outstanding role models. Her Girls Speak Out train-the-trainer program was successfully piloted by the YWCA Toronto in 2004, and certified Girls Speak Out programs are now being held throughout Canada.

Currently, Andrea is working on a project called The Caged Bird Sings*, focusing on girls in extreme circumstances, such as incarceration, sexual and physical abuse, child prostitution, armed conflict, and HIV/AIDS. She will launch The Caged Bird Sings Train-the-Trainers project in Africa.

Andrea has appeared in a Lifetime documentary called *I Am Beautiful*, on CNN's *Talk Back Live*, and on local and national radio and television shows in the USA. She has done online interviews and chat rooms with Parent Soup and AOL. She has been the keynote or featured speaker at YWCA youth conferences, on college campuses, at Rotary events, for parenting organizations, and in the General Assembly and Trusteeship Council of the United Nations.

Mother to a son, Jesse, and godmother to her niece, Yulahlia, Andrea lives in the San Francisco Bay Area.

*Used with the permission of Dr. Maya Angelou

Index

D

E

F

G